P9-CRE-046

AMERICA The BEAUTIFUL

ILLINOIS

By R. Conrad Stein

Consultants

Alice Jurica, Ed.D., Director, Bureau of Social Studies, Chicago Public Schools

Carl Oblinger, Head, Office of Research and Education, Illinois State Historical Library, Springfield

Robert L. Hillerich, Ph.D., Bowling Green State University, Bowling Green, Ohio

CHILDRENS PRESS®
CHICAGO

The Wrigley Building and the Chicago River at night

Project Editor: Joan Downing
Assistant Editor: Shari Joffe
Design Director: Margrit Fiddle
Typesetting: Graphic Connections, Inc.
Engraving: Liberty Photoengraving

3 4 5 6 7 8 9 10 R 96 95 94 93 92 91 90 89 88

Library of Congress Cataloging-in-Publication Data

Stein, R. Conrad.
America the beautiful, Illinois.

(America the beautiful state books)
Includes index.
Summary: Introduces the geography, history, government, economy, industry, culture, historic sites, and famous people of this Midwestern state.
1. Illinois—Juvenile literature. [1. Illinois]
I. Title. II. Series.
F541.3.S73 1987 977.3 86-9647
ISBN 0-516-00459-X

The Old Water Tower, one of the few buildings that survived the Great Chicago Fire

TABLE OF CONTENTS

Chapter 1

IN PRAISE OF ILLINOIS

IN PRAISE OF ILLINOIS

"How will it play in Peoria?" This question was asked in the days of vaudeville when singers, dancers, and other entertainers performed in traveling musical shows. Vaudevillians reasoned that if the citizens of a typical Midwest town such as Peoria, Illinois liked their show it would probably sell to the entire nation. If Peorians disliked it, the show was doomed to failure.

This "Peoria test" can still be applied to the Illinois community. Illinoisans' attitudes and prejudices, likes and dislikes, mirror those of Americans across the land. Perhaps this is true because of Illinois' central location; it is a crossroads between east and west, north and south. Or perhaps it is because Illinoisans come from such diverse backgrounds and follow such a wide variety of lifestyles.

As the central state of Midwest America, Illinois belongs to what is called the heartland of the country. Its economy is based on the production of both factories and fields. Its people originate from every spot on the globe. Its history has moments of glory and moments of shame. The state has been the home of poets and pioneers, political leaders and political hacks, and one of the truly great men in world history. Above all, the Illinois story reflects the ever-changing nature of America. A verse from the Illinois state song captures this sentiment well:

> Not without thy wondrous story. . .
> Can be writ the nation's glory, Illinois, Illinois.

Chapter 2

THE LAND

THE LAND

"At first, when we were told of these treeless lands, I imagined that it was a country ravaged by fire, where the soil was so poor it could produce nothing. But we have certainly observed the contrary; and no better soil can be found. . . ." So wrote Louis Jolliet, who with Father Jacques Marquette led the first group of European explorers to come upon the region now called Illinois.

Illinois spreads over 56,400 square miles (146,082 square kilometers). This makes it twenty-fourth in size among the states. Its longest distance from north to south is 385 miles (620 kilometers); its greatest distance from east to west is 218 miles (351 kilometers).

Much of Illinois is almost tabletop flat. Large areas of rugged hills are found only in the far south and in the northwest corner of the state. Most modern travelers race through Illinois on superhighways built for speed, not for scenery. When those highways veer away from the cities, they cut through mile after mile of windswept cornfields dotted by solitary farmhouses. Travelers complain that it's too flat—that the scenery is monotonous. But people who live in the state know better. There is great variety in the Illinois landscape, though it cannot be seen by those who hurry across the state on expressways. Illinois' surprising beauty is a gift to be discovered only by those who pause long enough to explore the back roads.

During pioneering times, prairie land like this covered more than half the state.

THE PRAIRIES

About ten thousand years ago, the last of four glaciers retreated north from America's heartland. At one time or another, glaciers covered 90 percent of what is now Illinois. These masses of ice, which sometimes towered a mile high, advanced relentlessly over the land, grinding down mountains and burying valleys. In their wake, the glaciers left sprawling flatlands. The tall grasses that later grew on this level country created the fertile plains that European explorers called prairies.

During pioneering times, prairie land made up more than half the state. Illinois prairie grasses grew so high and so thick they could hide a full-grown man or even a horse. A host of animals including bison, deer, elk, wolves, and foxes lived on the prairies. Above the tall grasses, the air was alive with the songs of thousands of birds. Illinois-born poet Carl Sandburg expressed his feelings for the state's grasslands in these words:

> The prairie sings to me in the
> forenoon and I know in the night
> I rest easy in the prairie arms,
> on the prairie heart.

Illinois is known as the Prairie State even though that nickname probably should have been given to Iowa or Nebraska. Unlike those states, which once were unbroken seas of grass, Illinois had some woodlands alongside its many rivers, and was heavily forested in the east and south. But it was in Illinois that westbound travelers first encountered the amazing fields of tall grasses, and the Prairie State name endured.

Scientists still differ about what conditions contributed to the formation of prairies. Why did the forests of early America end in eastern Illinois and suddenly give way to tall grasses? Some scientists claim that the prairie developed because of a subtle difference in rainfall. Others say the prairies were perpetuated by Indians who burned off dry grasses in the fall in order to flush out wild animals.

Pioneer farmers plowed up the prairie grasses in order to plant crops. Today, only tiny sections of original prairie remain. Goose Lake Prairie, a state natural area near Chicago, has been preserved to retain, as much as possible, its original prairie ecology. Visitors to the prairie can hike over trails and imagine the time when green and wine-colored tall grasses spread like an endless ocean from horizon to horizon.

RIVERS AND LAKES

The Illinois state song opens with the words: "By thy rivers gently flowing, Illinois, Illinois." Some five hundred rivers and streams flow through the state. And it is in the valleys created by these rivers that a traveler can find the stark beauty and surprising variety of landscape in the Prairie State. Along many of the back roads that hug the banks of streams are rocky bluffs painted white by the winds, groves of stately pine trees standing

The Mississippi River, shown here near Chester, forms the entire western border of Illinois.

like silent sentinels, and cool gullies carved by tumbling waters.

The Mississippi River forms the entire western border of the state. The southern and southeastern borders are made up of the Ohio and Wabash rivers. Other rivers are the Illinois, Rock, Vermilion, Fox, Des Plaines, Chicago, Sangamon, Spoon, Embarras, Big Muddy, Kaskaskia, Kankakee, Pecatonica, Calumet, and Kishwaukee.

Because of its flat terrain, Illinois has few large lakes. In fact, some of the state's biggest lakes are man-made. Lake Carlyle in south-central Illinois was created by a dam on the Kaskaskia River. Covering 26,000 acres (10,522 hectares), Carlyle is the largest lake lying wholly within the state. Rend Lake, also man-made, lies near the city of Mount Vernon in southern Illinois. Local people boast of the marvelous fishing at this popular recreation spot.

About sixty miles (ninety-six kilometers) of Lake Michigan shoreline forms the northeastern border of Illinois. In the center of this shoreline rise the glittering glass and steel buildings of modern Chicago.

Some Chicago blizzards bury the city and paralyze traffic.

CLIMATE

"If you don't like the weather here, just wait a minute; it'll change." That time-worn saying, Chicagoans are convinced, originated in their city. Certainly it describes Chicago's fickle weather. The entire state, in fact, is subject to sudden and sometimes violent weather changes. A fine summer day can explode into a thunderstorm with torrential rains and pelting hailstones. During winter, temperatures can plunge radically overnight. Without warning, a blizzard can bury a city and paralyze traffic. These extreme shifts in weather conditions are caused largely by the flat landscape. With no mountains to serve as barriers, winds sweep into the state in full force, bringing fair weather or foul.

Generally, the southern half of the state has milder winters than the north. Yet weeks and weeks of below-freezing temperatures during the winter months are common even in the city of Cairo at the state's extreme southern tip. Winters in the northern areas are not only intensely cold, but can last into April. Chicago is one of the few Major League cities where opening-day baseball games are occasionally called off due to snowstorms.

A rainbow shines through a summer storm near Peoria.

Through the course of a year, Illinoisans experience blistering heat followed by bone-chilling cold. The record high and low temperatures recorded in the state demonstrate this. In January, 1930, the northern town of Mount Carroll recorded a temperature of minus 35 degrees Fahrenheit (minus 37.2 degrees Celsius). On one July day in 1954, the people of East St. Louis in southern Illinois sweltered through a temperature reading of 117 degrees Fahrenheit (47.2 degrees Celsius).

On the farmlands, winds can be either friend or foe. During the summer months, prairie breezes are a delight. Tornadoes, however, can howl over the plains with such fury that houses are torn from their foundations. In fact, tornadoes have caused more deaths in Illinois than in any other state. In the winter, the combined forces of low temperatures and powerful winds produce wind-chill factors as low as minus 80 degrees Fahrenheit (minus 62.2 degrees Celsius).

In Illinois, rainfall affects many residents besides farmers. Floods are a constant threat to the people living along the state's many rivers. Spring flooding is an almost annual event at one river or another in Illinois. After a flood struck in the spring of 1985, one southern Illinois man shoveling mud out of his kitchen told a reporter, "If you're living on the river you almost have to

The Ozark Mountains extend from Missouri into southern Illinois to form the rugged Shawnee Hills (above). Apple River Canyon (right) is in the Driftless Area in the northwest corner of the state. The flat land of central Illinois, once covered with tall prairie grasses, now contains some of the richest agricultural soil in the world (below).

take it like a muskrat. You build and rebuild." Droughts can strike some areas, but they are generally nuisances rather than disasters.

TOPOGRAPHY

Illinois' topography (the shape of the land) can be divided into three regions—the northern, the central, and the southern.

Most of the northern third of Illinois is flat land. The dramatic exception is Jo Daviess County in the northwest corner of the state. Very little of that region was ever crossed by glaciers. Geologists call it the Driftless Area. In Jo Daviess County, rocky highlands jut skyward in defiance of the image of the Prairie State. Illinois' highest point, Charles Mound, which rises 1,235 feet (376 meters) above sea level, is there.

Central Illinois is the soul of the state's farm country. The same flat land that once supported tall prairie grasses now contains some of the richest agricultural soil in the world. But not all present-day farmland in central Illinois was prairie. Some of the farm country, especially in the east or along the rivers, was once forestland that was cleared by settlers more than 150 years ago.

The level prairies end in the southern third of the state. Most of the south was untouched by glaciers and features gentle hills and rocky glens. The Ozark Mountains extend from Missouri into southern Illinois to form the Shawnee Hills, a rugged region sometimes called the Illinois Ozarks. The first white settlers found that deer, elk, and buffalo were plentiful in these forested hills. After suffering through a terrible winter in 1830, however, the pioneers dubbed the area Egypt, after the biblical land of misery.

The hardy settlers who arrived in southern Illinois during the early 1800s were the vanguard of the millions of people who now call Illinois their home.

Chapter 3

THE PEOPLE

THE PEOPLE

A town called Silvis lies in northwestern Illinois near the Mississippi River. Its most famous feature is a short roadway with the unusual name Hero Street.

Around the turn of the century, immigrants from Mexico began working as laborers in Silvis's freight yards. The newcomers were so poor that at first they had to live in boxcars. But by the 1920s, many of them had saved enough money to buy modest houses in the town. A Mexican community sprang up along Second Street. "In the old days, all the mothers in the neighborhood called all the boys *hijos* [sons]. That's how close we were," recalls an elderly woman resident.

In the 1940s and 1950s, the sons of Silvis marched off to war. Second Street, which was only a block and a half long, sent fifty-seven young men to battlefields in World War II and the Korean conflict. According to Defense Department data, no area of comparable size contributed more fighting men to the two wars. Many of the second-generation Mexican Americans won medals for bravery. Eight of them never returned; they were killed in action.

It is no wonder, then, that in 1971 Second Street was renamed Hero Street. A monument now commemorates those who died far from home. Including the Vietnam War, seventy-eight men from twenty-two families living on Hero Street served in the military.

On Veterans Day, flags deck the houses of the street and flutter over the monument.

The Mexican Americans of Silvis are one part of the ethnic mosaic of Illinois. The United States is a country in which people from many nations have gathered and managed to live together. Certainly Illinois is a state in which people of every skin color, every religion, and every national origin now live and work.

POPULATION

According to the 1980 census, Illinois had 11,427,414 residents. In 1987, it was announced that Florida had replaced Illinois as the fifth most-populous state. Illinois now ranks sixth. Between 1970 and 1980, the state's population grew at the rate of 2.8 percent. The overall population gain in the United States for the same period was 11.45 percent. This means that Illinois is slowly losing population in relation to the country as a whole. The same is true of many other midwestern states; people continue to migrate to the warm states of the south and southwest.

The 1980 census also revealed that about 6 percent of Illinois residents were foreign-born. Poles, Germans, and Mexicans are currently among the largest of the foreign-born groups. Many people from Asian countries also have moved to the state in the past two decades. Most of the foreign-born residents live in urban areas. A spin of the dial on a Chicago radio will reveal programs in Spanish, Polish, Greek, and German.

Though the first Chicago settler was a black man, few blacks lived in the state before the Civil War. Even in 1910, blacks in Illinois numbered only 110,000 and lived mainly in the southern counties. Then the demand for industrial workers created by World Wars I and II triggered a mass migration of blacks from the

The diversity of Illinoisans' religious preferences reflects the diversity of the people themselves. Shown here are an Easter celebration in the Pilsen neighborhood of Chicago (far right), a bas mitzvah at North Shore Congregation Israel in Glencoe (top right), and the Ukrainian Eastern Orthodox Saints Volodymyr and Olha Church (bottom right).

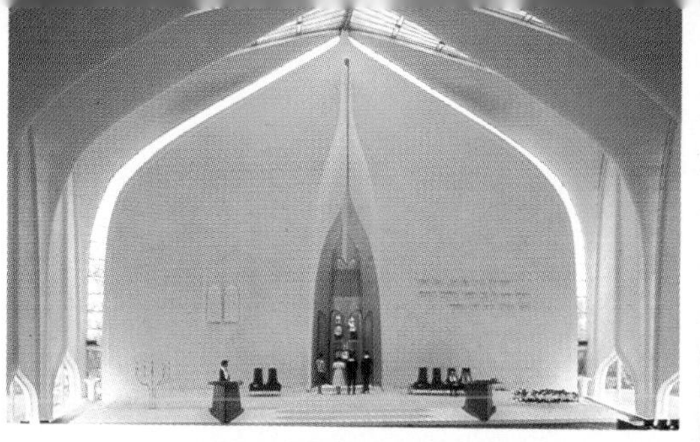

South to Illinois factory centers. In 1980, more than 14 percent of the state's population and 39 percent of the people of Chicago were black.

Religious preferences within Illinois reflect the ethnic diversity of the people. About one third of the population is Roman Catholic. Other large Christian groups include Presbyterians, Methodists, Baptists, Lutherans, and members of the United Church of Christ. A large number of Jewish synagogues and Eastern Orthodox Churches can be found in the major cities, as well as some Muslim mosques. There are also people who follow the teachings of Buddha.

POPULATION DISTRIBUTION

During Abraham Lincoln's time, most Illinoisans lived on farms or in tiny towns. But after the Civil War, railroad expansion and the growth of industry spurred a population explosion in the cities. Today, 83 percent of the population lives in urban areas.

Seven million people, more than 60 percent of the state's population, live in the Greater Chicago area alone.

By far the largest number of people live in the northern third of the state. Major population centers in this region are Chicago; Rockford, the state's second-largest city; and the Quad Cities area, which includes Moline, East Moline, Rock Island, and the Iowa city of Davenport. The largest central-Illinois cities are Springfield, the state capital; Peoria, the third-largest city; Champaign-Urbana, site of the downstate campus of the University of Illinois; and Decatur. In mainly rural southern Illinois, the largest urban center is the cluster of towns across from St. Louis, Missouri on the Illinois side of the Mississippi River.

Throughout the state are farming communities, some so tiny they do not even appear on road maps. Illinois' rich black earth continues to keep many people employed on farms, as it did in Abraham Lincoln's time. But today—whether by choice or necessity—the vast majority of Illinoisans live in the cities.

REGIONALISM

Not long ago, an army captain reviewed a company of new recruits, most of whom came from the Midwest. As the captain passed among the ranks of young soldiers, he asked each one which state he came from. "Kansas, sir!" "Nebraska, sir!" came the brisk replies. But one private hesitated at the question, thought hard, and finally answered, "Chicago, sir!" To this Chicago soldier, Illinois was a secondary location hardly worthy of mention.

Regionalism is a very real element of Illinois life. Its origins lie deep in the state's history. Southern Illinois was settled early, mainly by Virginians and Kentuckians. The people who originally

Sheepshearing demonstrations are among the Naper Settlement activities that help Naperville residents stay in touch with their rural heritage.

migrated to northern Illinois came from New England and New York. Their values conflicted with those of people living in the south. When the two streams of migration came together in central Illinois, tensions were created as each jockeyed for position in local government.

Even today, casual travelers in the state quickly notice its regionalism. In the north, especially in Chicago, one can hear accents from all over the world. In central and southern Illinois, the drawl is distinctly southern. In northern Illinois, rock music drifts from open car windows, whereas in the south, musical tastes tend toward country. A sign on a Chicago restaurant advertises sandwiches made on "croissants." In Cairo, those same sandwiches are made on "horseshoe rolls."

Chicagoans are among the most blatant of the regionalists. To them, the lands south of U.S. Route 80 are "downstate," and therefore foreign territory. Chicagoans who wish to go out of town for a weekend of fishing rarely go downstate, even though the fishing there is excellent. Instead they travel to lakes in Wisconsin. Why? Because Chicagoans *always* do their fishing there, that's why.

Some downstaters live their entire lives without ever visiting Chicago, with its crush of people.

Downstaters are just as wary of Chicago. They are not accustomed to the furious pace of city life. They fear street crime. Reports of political corruption disturb them. Some downstaters live their entire lives without ever visiting Chicago. Most follow the baseball exploits of the St. Louis Cardinals rather than the Chicago Cubs or White Sox.

Regionalism extends into politics. Cook County has a heavy concentration of Democratic voters, while the outlying counties and central Illinois generally vote Republican. Southern Illinois votes Democratic. The north has the greater population and the greater wealth. Chicago sometimes dominates the state politically, and when that happens, downstaters resent being pushed aside by the big-city kingpins. Governor Otto Kerner, who served in the 1960s, was closely aligned with Chicago's powerful mayor Richard J. Daley. Kerner often heard downstate critics claim, "When the head nods in Chicago, the tail wags in Springfield."

Many other states have regional differences, and certainly the split between north and south poses no insurmountable problem today. But regionalism has been a significant issue in the past. It is one of the elements that makes Illinois history a fascinating study.

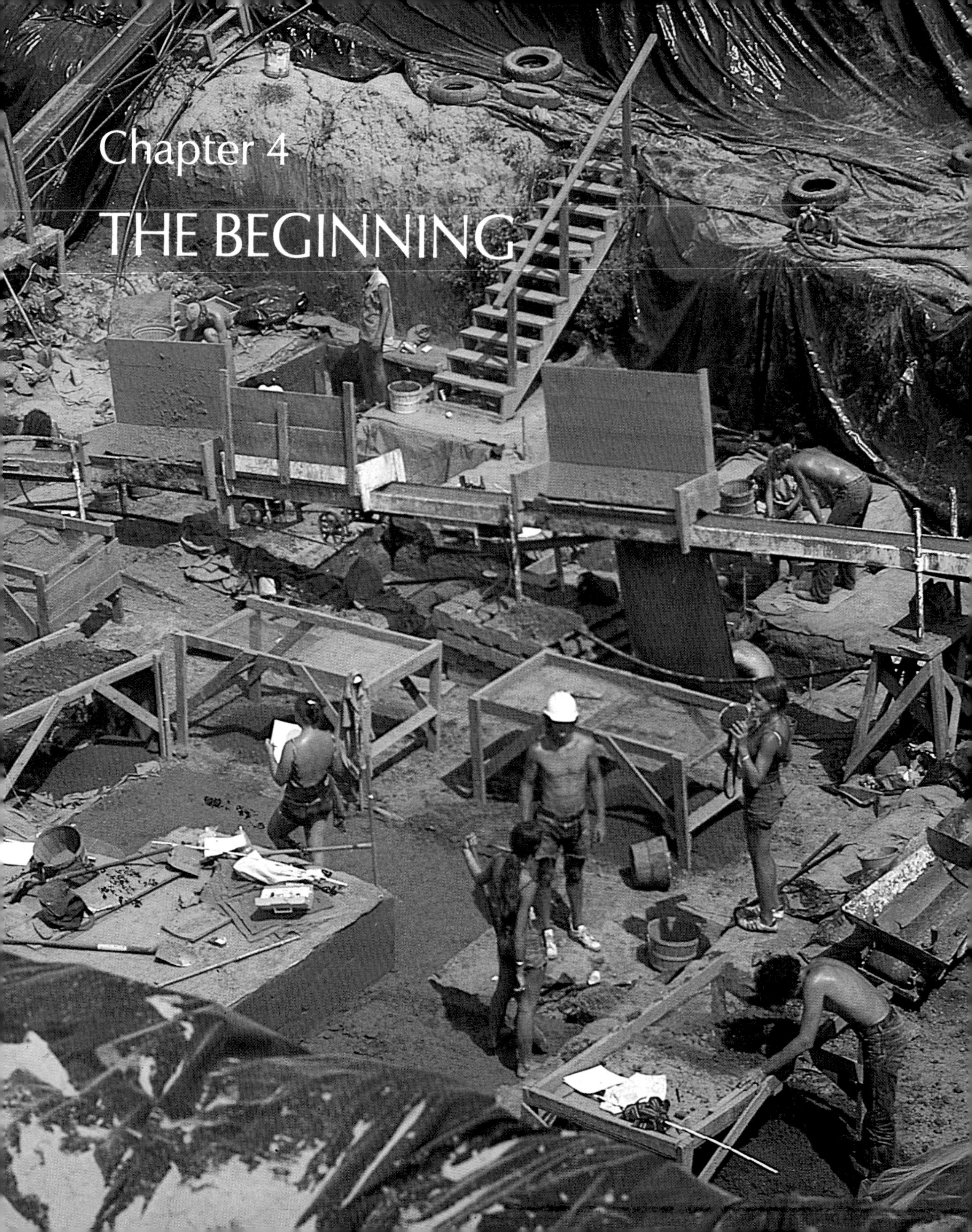

Chapter 4

THE BEGINNING

THE BEGINNING

In an astonishingly short period of time, Illinois was transformed from a frontier territory to a center of economic and political strength. The story of the state's remarkable progress is filled with surprises and examples of heroism.

THE ORIGINAL ILLINOISANS

Early man entered what is now Illinois almost on the heels of the last retreating glacier. In fact, the Indians of the region told legends about an ice god who once roared down from the north and froze the entire world. The first known people in Illinois were hunters and gatherers who left little evidence of their civilization.

Between 300 B.C. and A.D. 500, Indians of the Hopewell Culture flourished in the Middle West. Thousands of Hopewellian earthwork burial mounds were built on scattered sites throughout the region. Many of the Illinois mounds have been excavated. A fascinating display of some of these excavations can be found at Dickson Mound State Museum near Lewistown in central Illinois.

Mound Builders of the Mississippi Culture lived in Illinois from A.D. 800 to 1500. The Mississippians were an advanced people who built great cities, usually along riverbanks. Their mounds were used as places of worship rather than as burial sites. Many of their mounds were shaped like flat-topped pyramids, indicating

Monk's Mound (right), built by Mound Builders of the Mississippi Culture, is the largest earthwork in the world.

that the Mississippians probably had some contact with the sophisticated civilizations of Mexico and Central America. Monk's Mound at Cahokia near East St. Louis was the center of worship for a city that may have held as many as one hundred thousand people at the height of its development.

The mound-building cultures died out in the 1500s. Since they had no written language, we know few details about their lives. We do know that the late Mound Builders were extensive travelers. Jewelry and tools from both the Gulf of Mexico area and the Rocky Mountains have been found in their ruins. We also know they were ambitious builders. The remains of about ten thousand mounds have been identified in Illinois alone. Some have been carefully preserved by archaeologists; others stand in the middle of farm fields, surrounded by grazing cows.

THE ILLINIWEK

The people who gave their name to the state of Illinois lived in the area after the decline of the Mississippi Culture. The Illiniwek, meaning "the men" or "the superior men," were a confederation of several groups of Indians who spoke an Algonquian tongue.

For the Indians of Illinois, hunger was rarely a problem. Game was plentiful and rivers swarmed with fish.

They lived primarily along the streams and rivers, where they built long, narrow houses with birch frames covered by mats of woven grass and mud. At the time, the prairies teemed with game and rivers swarmed with fish. On the fertile plains the Illiniwek grew corn, squash, and pumpkins.

Life in the bountiful prairies would have been relatively easy for the Illiniwek had it not been for constant wars with their neighbors. For most North American Indians, intertribal warfare was an accepted way of life. But a development taking place hundreds of miles from their homes intensified the problems of the Illiniwek.

By the early 1600s, European enclaves along the East Coast had dramatically altered the Indian economy in all of North America. The Europeans had goods coveted by the Indians—guns, iron pots and pans, and knives. To obtain these goods, the Indians traded the pelts of fur-bearing animals such as beaver. When the fur-bearing animals grew scarce in the East, Indian trappers sought fresh hunting grounds farther west. By the mid-1600s, the fierce Iroquois began to invade the territory traditionally held by the Illiniwek. So the presence of Europeans on the continent affected the lives of the Illiniwek long before an actual European arrived in their midst.

THE EARLY FRENCH

"Thus we left the [familiar] waters . . . to float on those that would thenceforward take us through strange lands." With those words written in their journal in the year 1673, a band of seven Frenchmen left their outposts in Canada and plunged into the unexplored wilderness north of Illinois. The Frenchmen hoped to discover and chart the huge river that the Indians called Messipi—The Father of All the Waters.

The mission was led by a soldier, Louis Jolliet, and a priest, Father Jacques Marquette. The explorers made contact with the Illiniwek, who welcomed them, hoping these Frenchmen would drive away the Iroquois. Jolliet left this description of the untouched Illinois streams and prairies: "The [Illinois] River . . . seemed to me the most beautiful, and most suitable for settlement. . . . The river is wide and deep, abounding in catfish and sturgeon. Game is abundant there; buffalo, stags, does, and turkeys were found there in great numbers. . . . There are prairies . . . surrounded by forests of the same extent; beyond these the prairies begin again."

After Marquette and Jolliet came French soldiers who built forts, and black-robed priests who established missions. The person most successful at establishing French control of the area was explorer Sieur de La Salle. In 1680, La Salle built a fort on the Illinois River near the present-day site of Peoria. He placed another Illinois River fort on a magnificent wind-washed bluff that today is called Starved Rock.

By the early 1700s, French villages had sprung up along the Mississippi River in southern Illinois. Many Frenchmen married Indian women, though some brought their European wives to the wilderness settlements. History does not record the name of the

Each year, modern-day *voyageurs* such as these reenact segments of the Marquette-Jolliet voyage of exploration.

first European woman who came to the region. At some point during the early settlement period, the French shortened the term Illiniwek Territory to Illinois, and the name endured.

ILLINOIS BECOMES AMERICAN

In the first half of the 1700s, Illinois was part of a huge territory claimed by the king of France and called Louisiana. But the French grand plan to establish an empire in the central part of North America ended in 1763 with their defeat in the French and Indian War. The British, as victors in that war, gained control over what is now America's heartland.

Britain, however, never had enough soldiers to occupy this remote and wild region. When the American revolutionary war broke out, the British tried to make up for the lack of manpower by enlisting Indians to fight for their cause. From outposts in Illinois, British-armed Indians attacked American settlements in what was then the frontier region of Kentucky. To combat the raids, the Americans turned to George Rogers Clark, a seasoned Indian fighter who became a genuine hero in American history.

Under Clark's leadership, a small group of frontiersmen called the Big Knives left Kentucky to carry the war into enemy territory. In one of the most courageous marches in American history, the men climbed over trackless mountains and waded through waist-deep swamps. When they finally reached the banks of the Mississippi, Clark's men captured the Illinois settlements that the British had been using as supply posts. Clark's incredible victory helped gain Illinois and the surrounding regions for the infant republic of America.

During a twenty-year span, Illinois had been claimed by the French, the British, and finally the Americans. The ultimate victims of this international power struggle were the Illiniwek. The presence of white people intensified the Indian wars, and by the early 1800s, the Illiniwek were forced to move beyond the Mississippi River to try their luck in new lands to the west. They must have fared badly, for the group simply disappeared. No one knows where or when the last member of the once-proud Illiniwek people died.

THE NORTHWEST TERRITORY

At the end of the revolutionary war, Britain ceded to the United States all of its possessions south of Canada and east of the Mississippi. For the fledgling American government, this was a staggering acquisition of land. One massive region that became part of the spoils of war was the Northwest Territory, which included the present-day states of Ohio, Indiana, Illinois, Michigan, Wisconsin, and part of Minnesota.

Under the leadership of George Rogers Clark, a small group of frontiersmen climbed over rugged mountains and waded through waist-deep swamps to reach the banks of the Mississippi River and capture the Illinois settlements that the British had been using as supply posts during the American revolutionary war.

Above: American-appointed Potawatomi "chief" Shabbona
Below: Fort Massac was the starting-off point for George Rogers Clark's Illinois expedition.

With General "Mad Anthony" Wayne in command, the United States Army won a decisive victory over the Indians in the 1794 Battle of Fallen Timbers.

At first, the federal government had no master plan concerning the development of the land it had won from Britain. Originally, various eastern states had laid claim to parts of the Northwest Territory. The Illinois region, for example, became a county of Virginia.

Congress finally decided on a sound policy in 1787, when it passed the Northwest Ordinance. The ordinance was one of the most brilliant acts of legislation in American congressional history. Its terms did much to encourage the settlement of the region. The Northwest Ordinance prohibited slavery in the Northwest Territory; guaranteed all settlers the right to trial by jury and freedom of religious worship; encouraged education in the new land; drew rough boundaries of future states; and laid the ground rules for how these areas could become members of the Union. Most important, the ordinance declared that all new states admitted to the Union would have the same status as the original states.

But despite being so farsighted, the Northwest Ordinance did little to provide for the Indians who had lived on the land for generations. As settlers moved in, a bloody war exploded in the Northwest Territory.

General "Mad Anthony" Wayne was ordered to defeat the

Indians. He had received his nickname because of his many daredevil exploits during the revolutionary war. With Wayne in command, the United States Army scored a decisive victory over the Indians at the Battle of Fallen Timbers, fought in Ohio in 1794. After the battle, the Indians were forced to sign the Treaty of Greenville, which gave the government control of certain key areas in midwestern America. One of those areas was a swampy section of land on the shore of Lake Michigan near a river the Indians called "Checagou."

Most settlers had shown little interest in this marshland. In the late 1770s, however, a pioneer named Jean Baptiste Point du Sable built a log cabin on the riverbank and began trading with the Indians. Du Sable was a French-speaking black man who probably had been born in Haiti. His business prospered and du Sable steadily expanded his property. The land he owned was just west of what is now North Michigan Avenue in Chicago. Today it would be worth a fortune. Du Sable sold his store and left the area in 1800. The location of the trading post he had established was to become the center of a permanent Chicago settlement.

In 1803, the army built a post near du Sable's old settlement and called it Fort Dearborn. Certainly none of the men who hammered the fort's log walls together imagined that this muddy, unimpressive patch of weeds would soon become one of the world's great cities.

THE FORT DEARBORN MASSACRE

For nine uneventful years, Fort Dearborn stood at the spot where the sluggish Chicago River flowed into sparkling Lake Michigan. Several cabins clustered around it. One was owned by John Kinzie, a merchant who in 1804 took over what had been du Sable's trading post. Antoine Ouilmette, who is remembered for giving his name to the elegant Chicago suburb of Wilmette, also lived in the area. Fort Dearborn held about seventy soldiers; some forty civilians lived nearby.

The quiet life at the fort ended with the War of 1812. Once again, the British enlisted Indians to attack American frontier settlements. Fearful of an Indian siege, the territorial commander in Detroit sent word to the people in Fort Dearborn to march to the stronger post at Fort Wayne in present-day Indiana. It was a foolish order. Most historians believe that Fort Dearborn was strong enough to resist any siege the Indians could mount. Moreover, a friendly Potawatomi chief named Black Partridge had warned the whites that they might be attacked on their trip south along the lakefront.

On the blazing hot day of August 15, 1812, the troops, the civilians, and the Indian escorts of Fort Dearborn filed out of the huge log gate. Drummers tapped a cadence and fife players blew a lively tune. No one realized that the music would be a death march for many of them.

The column had advanced scarcely a mile over the sand dunes and through the groves of cottonwood trees when gunfire and war cries shattered the stillness. Suddenly, four hundred Potawatomi warriors descended on the settlers. The soldiers fought back with rifles, swords, and tomahawks. The wives of the soldiers wrestled with the Indians in desperate hand-to-hand struggles. Children threw rocks and hacked at the attackers with sticks. Captain William Wells, a veteran of Indian wars, fought with such fury that he later became a folk hero among the Potawatomi.

The whites, however, were hopelessly outnumbered. The battle lasted only fifteen minutes. Captain Nathan Heald, who

During the Fort Dearborn Massacre in 1812, Mrs. Nathan Heald (left), wife of the commander of the garrison, fought bravely and managed to survive. Captain William Wells (above), a veteran Indian fighter, was killed.

commanded the garrison, waved the white flag. His surrender failed to stop the slaughter. Men and women were hacked to death, and a few soldiers were captured and tortured. When the gunsmoke cleared, thirty-six soldiers, two women, and twelve children lay dead. John Kinzie's life had been spared because he had been friendly to the Indians. Chief Black Partridge managed to stop Indian warriors from taking even more lives, but Fort Dearborn was burned to the ground. The massacre at Fort Dearborn was one of the most grisly episodes in the settlement of northern Illinois. Years passed before pioneers dared to return to the place where the Chicago River spilled slowly into the gleaming waters of Lake Michigan.

Although the Fort Dearborn Massacre discouraged settlement in northern Illinois, settlers poured into the southern region. The frontier experience, an exciting chapter of the Illinois story, took place primarily in the southern and central portions of the state.

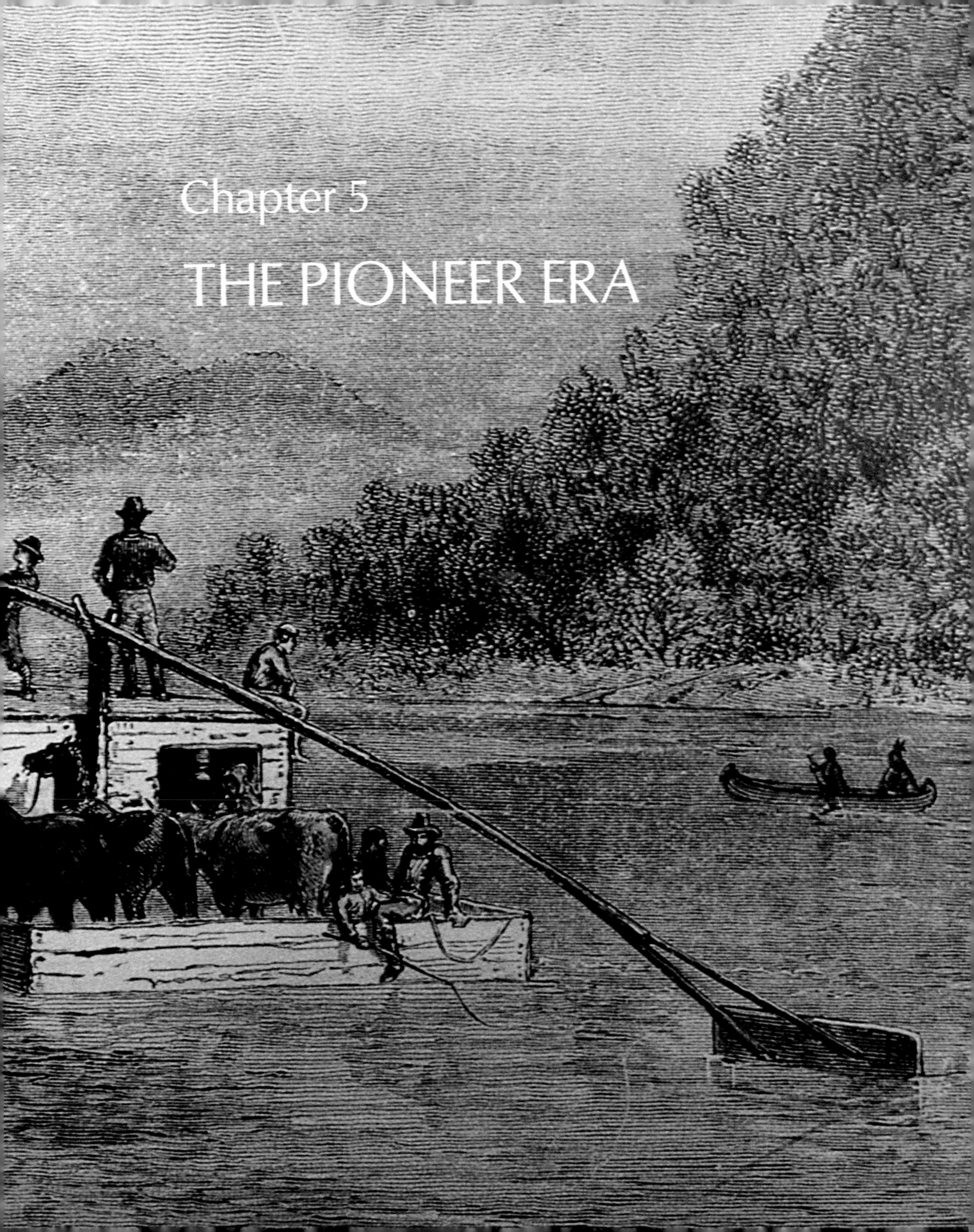

Chapter 5

THE PIONEER ERA

THE PIONEER ERA

Before he became the fifth president of the United States, James Monroe made two brief trips to the Illinois region. He claimed in a report that the land was "miserably poor," especially along the shoreline of Lake Michigan. He concluded that the area would "never contain a sufficient number of inhabitants to entitle [it to] membership in the confederacy." Monroe lived long enough to see Illinois become a booming young state. His children and grandchildren saw Illinois grow into one of the industrial and political giants of the nation.

STATEHOOD

The Northwest Ordinance stipulated that a proposed state had to reach a population of sixty thousand voters before it could enter the Union. Yet Illinois was admitted as the twenty-first state on December 3, 1818, even though its population numbered only about forty thousand voters. It achieved statehood early largely because of the efforts of Nathaniel Pope, the territorial delegate to Washington, D.C. and a powerful man in the federal government. Pope also used his influence to push the upper border of the state forty-one miles (sixty-six kilometers) farther north in order to give Illinois its own small corner of the Lake Michigan shoreline. At that time, no one could begin to guess how important that minor border adjustment would be to the future of the state. Had it not been for the border change, Chicago would now be part of Wisconsin.

At the time of statehood, only the southern third of Illinois was settled. The state's first capital was Kaskaskia, a town that had been founded by the French. It was there that delegates gathered to write Illinois' original constitution and to elect Shadrach Bond the first governor. After only two years, the capital was moved to the woodland community of Vandalia. Seventeen years later, the seat of government was transferred again, this time to its present site at Springfield.

LIFE ON THE ILLINOIS FRONTIER

Though the early pioneers knew they would face hardship and danger, they flocked to Illinois in the hope that their families would eventually enjoy a better life. For the overwhelming majority of settlers, the gamble paid off.

> Way down upon the Wabash
> Such land was never known;
> If Adam had passed over it,
> The soil he'd surely own;
> He'd think it was the garden
> He'd played in when a boy
> And straight pronounce it Eden,
> In the state of El-a-noy.

These words start a lively song sung by travelers as they journeyed to the new state. The majority of the early immigrants were southerners who pronounced the state's name "El-a-noy." Many of these pioneers looked upon this new region of rivers and shining prairies as the Promised Land they had read about in their

Pioneers from the southeast took horse-drawn wagons over the Cumberland Road to Illinois and stopped at inns such as this one on their way.

Bibles—the land of milk and honey that God once promised to Moses and the Hebrew children.

Immigrants from the Deep South came up the Mississippi in flatboats whose decks were crowded with cattle, pigs, horses, dogs, cats, chickens, and household furniture. Those from the southeast took horse-drawn wagons over the National Road (also called the Cumberland Road) that led from Cumberland, Maryland to Vandalia, Illinois. Few people from the populous northeastern region came to Illinois during the early pioneering era because of the enormous difficulty posed by crossing the Appalachian Mountains.

Many pioneer farmers carried a book called *Illinois As It Is,* written by Fred Gerhard. In one chapter, Gerhard advised the immigrants to bring "a pair of good horses, a wagon, a cow, a

A pioneer family that settled in forestland had to make a clearing before a cabin could be built or land could be plowed for farming.

couple of pigs, several domestic fowl, two plows . . . together with a few other tools and implements."

Building a house was an immigrant farmer's first task. Pioneer houses were usually one-room, windowless log cabins that had only the bare earth as a floor. Because of this, even the best housekeepers were forced to share their homes with spiders, crickets, and field mice.

Since they needed logs to build their cabins, most pioneers shunned the prairies and settled near the forests. But when the woodlands were fully occupied, settlers were forced to try farming on the prairies. At that time, it was widely believed that the treeless prairie land would not be fertile enough to support crops. But the new farmers quickly discovered that the prairie soil was rich beyond their dreams. Plowing the thick, gummy sod, however, was a frustrating chore. Wooden plows broke and the "gumbo," as the sod was called, clung stubbornly to iron plowshares. Then, in 1837, a young Illinois blacksmith named John Deere invented a new type of polished steel plow that cut effortlessly and cleanly through the prairie sod. Deere built a factory in the town of Moline to manufacture his new plows, and eventually became a millionaire.

The fertility of the black prairie soil so astounded farmers that they wrote excited letters to relatives who owned less-productive farms in other parts of the country. Thomas Lincoln, who had farmed in Kentucky and Indiana, received such a letter and decided to try his luck in Illinois. In 1830, he and his family, including his twenty-one-year-old son Abraham, moved to the state.

The most dangerous threat to a pioneer family was disease. Typhoid, cholera, and smallpox were dreaded killers that periodically ravaged early pioneer settlements. Two diseases that seemed to be endemic to the state were malaria, which the settlers knew as the "Illinois shakes," and "milk sickness," which was believed to be caused by drinking milk from a cow that had eaten poison weeds. The diseases struck children the hardest. One pioneer doctor lamented, "We never expect to raise any of our children, at least till they are seven or eight years old." The threat of deadly epidemics, however, could not stop the flow of hopeful farmers, as a verse from the "El-a-noy" song attests:

> She's crawfish in the swampy lands,
> The milk-sick and the shakes;
> But these are slight diversions
> And take not from the joy
> Of living in this garden land
> The state of El-a-noy.

A profound change in the immigration pattern occurred in 1825 with the completion of the New York State Erie Canal, which cut through the Appalachian Mountains. This opened the door to

The Illinois Central Railroad Company played a large part in attracting settlers to Illinois, the "Garden State of the West." Advertisements such as this one offered for sale rich farmland along the course of the rail line.

settlers from the East and to the many European immigrants arriving daily at the Port of New York. Illinois soon became a new home for thousands of Germans escaping the revolution that ravaged their homeland, and for throngs of Irish forced out of their country by the great potato famine. Most of these newcomers settled in the northern part of the state. Because their political and religious views were radically different from those of the people living in southern Illinois, the regionalism that pervades the state today began to take root.

The rush to settle northern Illinois, however, led to conflict with the Indians and spawned a tragic episode in the state's history.

THE BLACK HAWK WAR

The Rock River country in northwestern Illinois was once the exclusive territory of the Sauk and Fox Indians. When settlers entered this region, skirmishes broke out between them and the Indians. In 1831, the federal government ordered the Indians to move beyond the Mississippi River to Iowa. Most of the Fox and Sauk left immediately. Only the followers of a determined Indian leader named Black Hawk refused to be pushed off the land where they had been born. Finally, pressure from the United States Army forced even Black Hawk and his people to move west of the Mississippi.

The following spring, Black Hawk and about four hundred Sauk Indians recrossed the Mississippi. Although they wanted simply to plant corn in Wisconsin, frontier settlers believed that Black Hawk was on the warpath. The army was called in and an ugly war broke out. Both sides committed acts of savagery that included scalpings, the murder of women and children, and the torture of captives. An editorial in a Galena newspaper called for a "war of extermination until there shall be no Indian [with his scalp on] left in Illinois."

Facing a huge army, Black Hawk tried to retreat across the Mississippi. The last battle in the war was one of shocking cruelty. Black Hawk and his people were trapped with the Mississippi River at their backs and hundreds of soldiers in front of them. Though Black Hawk tried to surrender, the soldiers' fury had raged out of control. Troops set upon the Indians with clubs, knives, and guns. The massacre lasted eight hours. One observer claimed that the waters of the Mississippi River were "tinged with the blood of Indians."

The Black Hawk War closed the sad chapter of Indian history in

The Battle of Bad Axe on the shores of the Mississippi River (above) was the last battle in the Black Hawk War. Volunteer troops massacred hundreds of Sauk Indians and captured Sauk war chief Black Hawk (right).

Illinois. By the end of the 1830s, few Indian communities remained in the state. The original Illinoisans moved farther west while the relentless settlers took over the land the Indians had once called their own.

After the Black Hawk War, northern Illinois flourished. Chicago was incorporated as a city in 1837, and within two decades became the state's leading urban center. But while northern Illinois was growing and developing, the state and the American Union were being torn asunder over the most burning issue of the day—slavery.

Angered at Elijah Lovejoy's crusade against slavery, an unruly mob set fire to his warehouse and destroyed his printing press.

A HOUSE DIVIDED

In 1833, a young man named Elijah Lovejoy opened a small newspaper in St. Louis, Missouri. His paper regularly published editorials denouncing slavery as a monstrous institution. Because Missouri was a slave state, these editorials angered his neighbors. One night a group of men broke into Lovejoy's office and destroyed his printing press.

Lovejoy then moved his newspaper across the river to Alton, Illinois. He reasoned that in Illinois, a free state, he would find allies in his crusade against slavery. In its first editorial, the new *Alton Observer* declared, "The system of Negro slavery is an awful evil and sin." Shortly after the editorial ran, a mob ransacked Lovejoy's office, and as the St. Louis men had done, demolished his printing press.

Lovejoy quickly learned that even though Illinois was a free state, many of its citizens had little sympathy for abolitionists (those who wanted to end or abolish slavery). In fact, in 1837, the Illinois legislature passed a resolution condemning all abolitionist societies in the state. One of the few congressmen to vote against the resolution was a young state representative named Abraham Lincoln.

Despite the fact that threats were made against his life, Elijah Lovejoy was determined to continue his campaign against slavery. "I know that I have the right to freely speak and publish," he wrote. "You can crush me if you will; but I shall die at my post, for I cannot and will not forsake it. . . . If I fail, my grave shall be made in Alton."

One night, an unruly mob gathered with the intention of destroying yet another printing press belonging to the *Observer.* This time, Lovejoy and a few of his friends tried to defend his property. A volley of shots rang out, and Elijah Lovejoy fell dead.

Lovejoy's tragic story illustrates the bitter divisions the slavery issue caused within the state. The population of Illinois quadrupled between 1830 and 1850. Many of the newcomers—especially Germans and New Englanders—were violently opposed to slavery; their views clashed with those of the thousands of Illinois citizens who were sympathetic to the South. The divisions within the state mirrored those within America itself.

Into this violent conflict between pro-slavery and anti-slavery factions stepped the remarkable frontiersman Abraham Lincoln.

Lincoln, born into a struggling farm family, had little formal schooling. He hungered for learning, however, and devoured any book he could find. He worked at dozens of odd jobs, studied at night, and eventually became a lawyer. In court, he had the ability to argue a case so simply that even jurors who were poorly educated could understand his point of view. Yet he was just as skilled at presenting complicated legal issues to a highly educated judge.

The people of Illinois' log-cabin settlements genuinely liked Lincoln. His sense of humor was famous, and he never missed an opportunity to laugh at himself. When he entered politics, he soon was confronted with the explosive issue of slavery. Though Lincoln was not an abolitionist, he was opposed to slavery. "As I would not be a slave, so I would not be a master," he once said. Lincoln hoped that, given time, the institution of slavery simply would die a natural death. He did believe, however, that slavery should not be allowed to extend to the new states opening up in the West. On this matter, he clashed with a formidable opponent.

In 1858, Lincoln ran for the United States Senate against the powerful Illinois Democrat Stephen A. Douglas. To start his election drive, Lincoln delivered one of the most stirring speeches in the history of America. Standing in the old Capitol Building in Springfield, he declared: "A house divided against itself cannot stand. I believe this government cannot endure, permanently, half-slave and half-free."

The climax of Lincoln's campaign for the Senate was a series of seven face-to-face encounters with his opponent. The Lincoln-Douglas Debates, which took place in various Illinois cities, focused on the extension of slavery into the new states. During the debates, Lincoln demonstrated his quick mind, compelling speaking voice, and talent as a speech writer. Though he lost the

During the Lincoln-Douglas Debates (above left), cartoonists enjoyed depicting the physical contrast between the tall, lanky Abraham Lincoln (far left) and the short, rotund Stephen A. Douglas (above).
On February 11, 1861, President-elect Lincoln's Springfield neighbors gathered to wish him well as he left for Washington (below).

Five days after the Union victory in the Civil War, Lincoln (above) was shot and killed while attending a play at Ford's Theatre in Washington (below).

Senate race to Douglas, publication of the spirited debates gave him national recognition.

Lincoln was elected president of the United States in 1860. But the election left the country dangerously divided. Though Lincoln had easily won a majority of the electoral votes, he won only 40 percent of the popular vote. Furthermore, most of his popular votes came from the North.

As the president-elect left his home in Springfield for Washington on February 11, 1861, he told his neighbors: "Here I have lived for a quarter of a century, and have passed from a young man to an old man. Here my children have been born, and one is buried. I now leave not knowing when, or whether ever, I may return, with a task before me greater than that which rested upon Washington. Without the assistance of that Divine Being who ever attended him, I cannot succeed. With that assistance I cannot fail."

No president before or since has faced such peril immediately upon assuming office. When Lincoln took his oath, seven southern states had already seceded from the Union. A month later, Fort Sumter was fired upon by Confederate artillery, and the United States plunged into the most destructive war of its history. The president guided the Union forces through the war, emancipated the slaves, and won reelection in 1864. Then, only five days after Confederate General Robert E. Lee surrendered his armies, Lincoln was shot and killed.

Even his political enemies, and he had many, wept for the fallen president. But no one felt the loss more heavily than the people of Illinois. In Lincoln's home state, men and women grieved as they would for a departed father. Today, his tomb near Springfield attracts admirers who come to pay homage to this son of Illinois, one of history's greatest men.

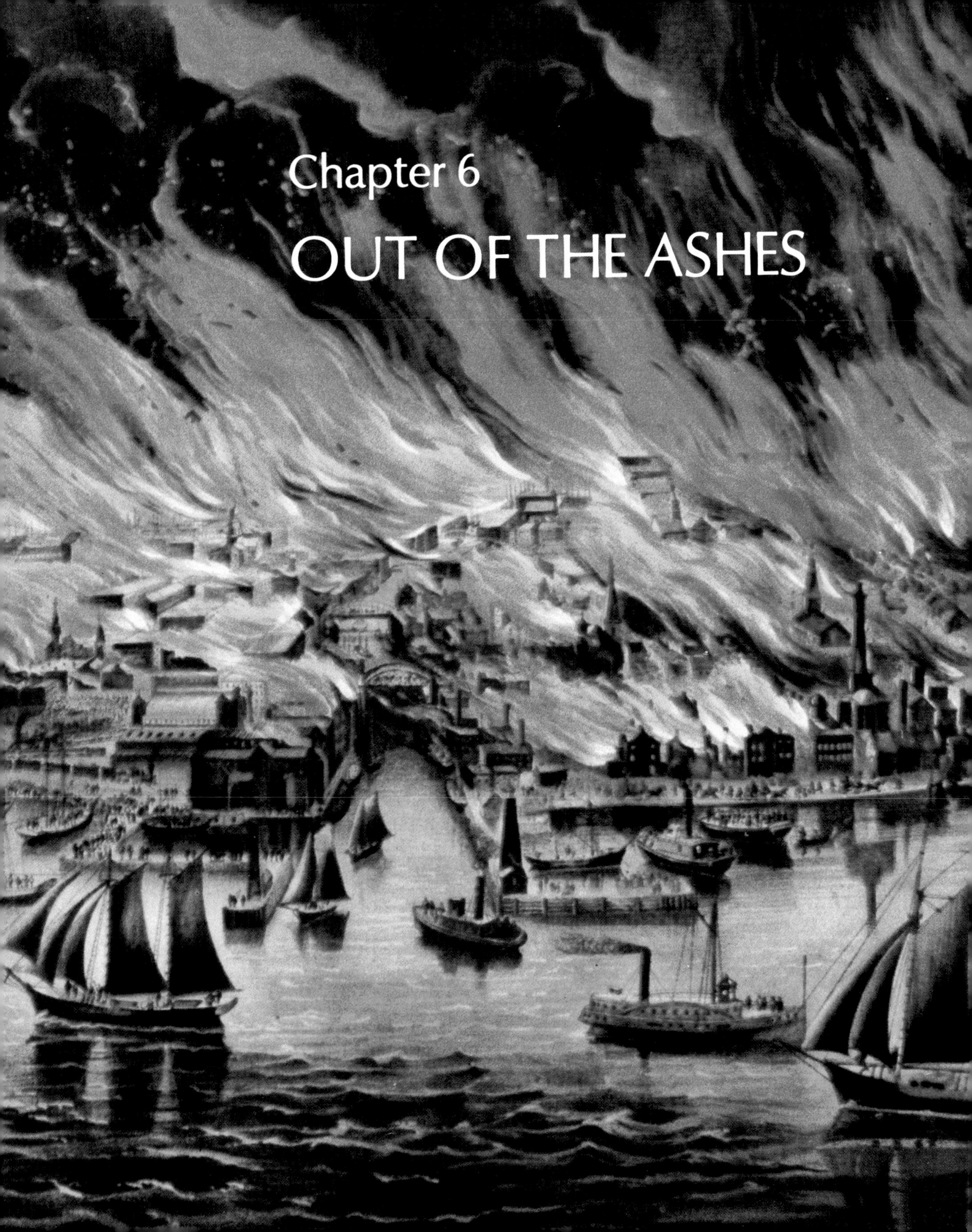

Chapter 6

OUT OF THE ASHES

OUT OF THE ASHES

During the pioneer era, most of the major events in Illinois took place in the southern and central regions of the state. After the Civil War, however, the focus shifted to the north. The dynamic city of Chicago began to dominate affairs of the state.

THE SECOND CITY

By 1870, Chicago's population had reached three hundred thousand, a threefold increase in only one decade. No other city in world history had grown with such astonishing speed. Its rapid expansion was primarily a result of the city's thriving transportation industry. Located at the national crossroads of east and west, Chicago was a natural railway hub. At the time of the Civil War, more than a hundred trains passed through the city each day. The slaughterhouses, factories, and lumberyards that sprang up created jobs, and people flocked to the city to fill them.

But for this fabulous growth Chicago paid a price. At least 90 percent of its houses were made entirely of wood. Many had been hammered together in only a few weeks. Factory buildings, warehouses, sidewalks, and even streets also were constructed of wood. In the dry months, Chicago was a tinderbox, and frightful fires devoured entire neighborhoods. Then, on the night of October 8, 1871, a fire struck that was so devastating many Chicagoans feared it was the end of the world.

Huge crowds tried to flee the flames of the Chicago Fire by crossing the Randolph Street bridge (left). The view above shows the destruction left in the wake of the fire.

The Great Chicago Fire began in a barn behind a house owned by Patrick O'Leary. For generations most Chicagoans believed that the fire started when a cow kicked over a lantern; Mrs. O'Leary, however, claimed from the beginning that there had been no lantern in the barn that night. A relentless wind whipped out over the prairies and drove the flames on. In less than two hours, the Chicago fire chief declared the blaze out of control. The flames jumped the south branch of the Chicago River and engulfed the downtown area. So intense was the whirlwind of fire that blasts of superheated air were felt a hundred miles across the lake at Holland, Michigan.

A throng of people fled through the Chicago streets in an attempt to escape from the advancing flames. At its peak, the fire raced through the town's buildings faster than a man can run. According to one eyewitness, "A column of flames would shoot up from a burning building, catch the force of the wind, and strike the next one. It was simply indescribable in its terrible grandeur."

In 1899, social worker Jane Addams (above) opened Hull House (left), a settlement facility founded to help the European immigrant laborers who had settled in Chicago.

The fire raged for more than twenty-four hours. In its wake it left the city in ashes. At least three hundred people were dead and about one hundred thousand were left homeless. Property damage was estimated at $200 million. But with remarkable speed, Chicago rose out of its ashes. New buildings were built on the ruins of the old. A rigid construction code required the new buildings to be made of brick, ending the tinderbox conditions that had prevailed in the past. In 1874, a British visitor who had walked down State Street observed, "It is difficult to realize the fact that the busy thoroughfare with its beautiful buildings . . . was but three years before a heap of charred ruins."

By the 1890s, Chicago had become the second largest city in the country and one of the great industrial centers of the world.

CAPTAINS OF INDUSTRY, KNIGHTS OF LABOR

Because Chicago was originally a swampland, in its early days the streets were mired in mud. To solve the drainage problem, city planners decided to raise the level of the streets. This was such an enormous engineering task that few construction companies dared to take it on. A young engineer named George Pullman, however, accepted the contract. Pullman successfully raised the streets and made money on the project, as well. He used his profits to form a company that made elegant railroad passenger cars. George Pullman became a multimillionaire.

Pullman was one of the many captains of industry who prospered in Illinois. Another was Cyrus McCormick, who invented ingenious farm implements and manufactured them in Chicago factory complexes. Philip D. Armour and Gustavus Swift earned fabulous fortunes by operating meat-packing companies on Chicago's South Side. Not all the industrialists were headquartered in Chicago. Plow-maker John Deere's largest plants were in Moline. Powerful coal-mine owners carried on their operations in southern Illinois.

These industrial tycoons were energetic, dynamic men whose talents brought thousands of jobs to the state. But many of them preserved their fortunes by paying very low wages to their workers. As a result, thousands of Illinois laborers lived in desperate poverty.

The Chicago slums at the end of the nineteenth century were disgraceful. Most of the slum dwellers were European immigrant laborers who were exploited by factory owners. In 1889, the famous social worker Jane Addams opened a settlement facility called Hull House in the heart of those slums. She described the surrounding neighborhood in these words: "The streets are

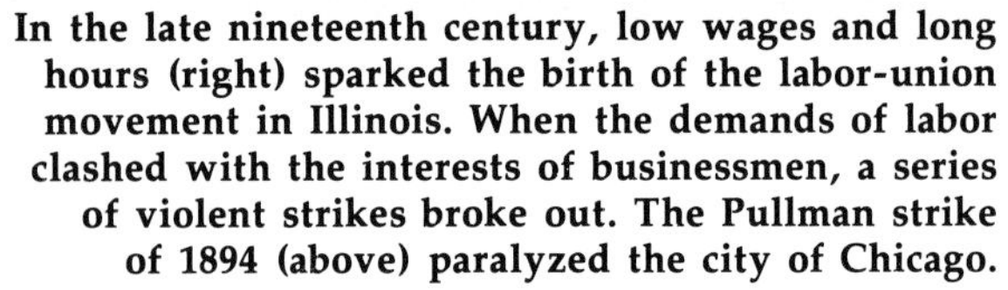

In the late nineteenth century, low wages and long hours (right) sparked the birth of the labor-union movement in Illinois. When the demands of labor clashed with the interests of businessmen, a series of violent strikes broke out. The Pullman strike of 1894 (above) paralyzed the city of Chicago.

inexpressibly dirty, the number of schools inadequate, sanitary legislation unenforced, and street lighting bad." Low wages and long hours sparked the birth of the labor-union movement in Illinois. The Knights of Labor, headquartered in Chicago, was an organization that fought for laws that would give the worker an eight-hour day and would eliminate child labor. Because the demands of the Knights of Labor clashed with the desires of the businessmen, a series of violent strikes rocked the state. Strikes broke out in the southern Illinois coal fields. Chicago was paralyzed in 1894 when railroad workers walked off their jobs to support a strike at the Pullman Palace Car Company.

A labor conflict that had lasting significance took place near Haymarket Square in Chicago on May 4, 1886. Police were trying to break up a peaceful labor rally at the square when a bomb exploded. As police and workers traded pistol fire, seven policemen and at least two civilians were killed. Eight radical

The Haymarket riot ended in tragedy when police tried to break up a peaceful labor rally in Chicago on May 4, 1886.

labor leaders were convicted of inciting violence. Four were hanged and one committed suicide in his jail cell. Seven years later, Illinois Governor John Peter Altgeld pardoned the remaining three labor leaders, convinced that they had received an unfair trial. Altgeld's action took great courage; the uproar over the pardoning ultimately cost him his political career.

Although the Haymarket tragedy temporarily discredited the labor movement in the eyes of the American public, European socialist groups sympathized with the workers involved in the incident. Since the riot had occurred in early May, they declared that May Day celebrations would henceforth commemorate the struggling workers of Chicago. Today, May Day is the most important workers' holiday in the European Communist world. The Soviet Union marks the occasion with a giant military parade and a spectacular fireworks display. Few Americans realize that the observance of this major international holiday for workers originated on the West Side of Chicago at Haymarket Square.

THE EARLY TWENTIETH CENTURY

Despite labor problems, Illinois was hailed as a progressive state as the country moved into the 1900s. It was the first state in the Union to pass a law requiring coal-mine owners to obey strict safety standards. The General Assembly approved a child-labor ordinance as early as 1891, and a workman's compensation act in 1911. Also in 1911, Illinois was the first state to pass "mother's-aid" legislation, authorizing money for the care of dependent or neglected children. Finally, in 1913, Illinois became the first state east of the Mississippi River to grant women the right to vote in presidential elections.

As industry prospered in Illinois, the state continued to be a magnet for newly arriving foreign immigrants. By 1910, Germans were the largest foreign-born group, followed by Austro-Hungarians, Poles, Scandinavians, Irish, and Italians. Most of these European immigrants settled in the northern cities, though a large number settled in such southern Illinois towns as Granite City, Belleville, Herrin, and Mount Olive. Half the people of Chicago, Joliet, and Rockford were foreign born. It was said that there were more Poles in Chicago than in Warsaw. Pulaski Day (October 11), which honors Polish-born revolutionary war hero Casimir Pulaski, is an especially important holiday in Illinois.

During the World War I years, many black people from the southern United States came to work in Illinois' industries. As blacks competed with impoverished whites for housing and jobs, ugly race riots broke out in several Illinois cities.

In East St. Louis, such a riot occurred in July of 1917. Its savagery shocked the nation. Black people were beaten and lynched and their homes were torched. At least fifty people were killed, and property damage totaled more than a million dollars.

As blacks competed with impoverished whites for jobs during World War I, ugly race riots broke out in several Illinois cities, including Chicago (above).

A race riot erupted in Chicago on a sweltering July day in 1919. Tensions had been running high because an originally small black neighborhood on the South Side had become overcrowded and blacks were beginning to move into previously all-white neighborhoods. A young black boy swimming in Lake Michigan inadvertently crossed an unmarked line into an area used by whites. When he tried to come ashore, irate whites threw rocks at the boy, forcing him to swim to deep water, where he drowned. Gangs, both white and black, took to the streets, firing at each other with pistols and shotguns. Fifteen whites and twenty-four blacks were killed during the riot, and hundreds were injured. Years were to pass before the tensions raised by racial violence eased.

PROHIBITION, DEPRESSION, AND WAR

When Americans traveling in Europe tell Europeans that they're from Chicago, the European response is often, "Ah, Al Capone." This is the legacy of 1920s Chicago. And because Hollywood delights in making Prohibition-era movies, that image may never die.

No law in American history was more openly violated than the law prohibiting the sale of alcoholic beverages. In the 1920s, illegal taverns called speakeasies operated in nearly every Chicago neighborhood. Underworld characters made fortunes providing hard liquor and beer. Chicago's most notorious beer baron was Alphonse Capone. By terrorizing rival gangs and bribing Chicago politicians, he gained a virtual monopoly over the illegal alcohol trade. A grisly mass murder took place on St. Valentine's Day, 1929, when Capone's henchmen gunned down seven members of the "Bugs" Moran gang in a North Side garage. The world press sensationalized the St. Valentine's Day Massacre and Chicago gained a reputation it has not been able to shake.

> Once I built a railroad, made it run
> Made it race against time,
> Once I built a railroad, now it's done.
> Brother, can you spare a dime?

This song was sung during the most bitter years of the Great Depression of the 1930s. Though the economic depression was a nationwide tragedy, it struck Illinois especially hard because of the state's dependence on heavy industry. As money became scarce, production dropped; as production dropped, employees were laid off. By 1933, more than 1.5 million Illinois workers were

Al Capone was Chicago's most notorious beer baron during the Prohibition era.

unemployed. Children went to school with holes in their shoes. Families used newspapers as blankets.

In the midst of the depression years, however, an unusual federal program called the Civilian Conservation Corps (CCC) helped to improve Illinois park and wilderness facilities. The CCC took jobless young men off the city streets and gave them useful tasks in the country. In Illinois, CCC members worked mainly in the state parks, where they cut hiking trails, built wooden bridges, and cleared camping areas. The fruits of their labor can be seen even today. The log cabins and the magnificent lodge at Starved Rock State Park, for example, were built with the help of CCC workers.

World War II quickly brought the country out of the economic depression. Because the war created a food shortage, Illinois farmers received higher prices for their crops. Industrial jobs, so scarce in the 1930s, suddenly were plentiful. Tanks and heavy equipment rolled out of the Peoria Caterpillar plant. The Rock Island area became the nation's leader in the production of ammunition and artillery. Southern Illinois coal mines churned out tons of coal and still could not meet orders. Giant factories in Chicago manufactured thousands of aircraft engines.

Enrico Fermi (right) headed a group of physicists who produced the first man-made nuclear chain reaction. A monument on the University of Chicago campus (above) commemorates the event.

World history was forever altered by one event that took place in Illinois during the war years. In December of 1942, a group of scientists headed by Italian physicist Enrico Fermi gathered in a secret laboratory under the stands of the University of Chicago football field and produced the first man-made nuclear chain reaction. This reaction proved that a powerful weapon fueled with uranium could be built, giving Illinois the ominous distinction of being the birthplace of the atomic bomb.

MODERN ILLINOIS

In 1948, voters elected Adlai Ewing Stevenson governor of Illinois. Stevenson was from an old and respected family from Bloomington, Illinois. His grandfather had been vice-president of the United States from 1893 to 1897. Stevenson's career as governor was not outstanding, but his speeches and writings showed intellect and wit. His sense of humor was demonstrated in a famous veto message meant to chastise the legislature for bothering to write a bill, promoted by bird lovers, that would require all Illinois cats to wear tiny bells strapped around their necks: "The problem of cat versus bird is as old as time. If we attempted to resolve it by legislation, who knows whether we may be called upon to take sides as well in the age-old problems of dog versus cat, bird versus bird, even bird versus worm?"

Stevenson's eloquence made him a popular national figure. The Democrats chose him as their presidential candidate in 1952 and again in 1956. Each time, he was defeated by war hero Dwight D. Eisenhower. Stevenson served as United States ambassador to the United Nations until his death in 1965. His son, Adlai III, represented Illinois in the United States Senate from 1970 to 1981.

The state's most powerful political figure in the 1960s and early 1970s was Chicago's mayor, Richard J. Daley. Daley delighted in his role as a "kingmaker" of the Democratic party. During the 1960 Democratic Convention, he played a major role in ensuring that John F. Kennedy was nominated as the party's candidate for president. He then helped his candidate win the presidential race by delivering a Chicago vote so enormous that it was able to carry Illinois for the Democrats even though many downstate Republicans voted against Kennedy. The losing candidate, Richard M. Nixon, bitterly denounced "vote fraud" in Chicago.

Daley served as mayor from 1955 until his death in 1976. During his administration, he withstood charges of nepotism, political corruption among his associates, and riots in black neighborhoods in the 1960s. His role in the 1968 Democratic Convention, which met in Chicago, will never be forgotten. Amid the gloom of the Vietnam War, a bloody clash took place between war protesters and police—a clash that Daley made no attempt to stop. With tear gas thick in the air, police beat protesters with nightsticks and dragged them to patrol wagons. Television cameras recorded the violence while the crowd of protesters

Prominent Illinois politicians include Adlai Stevenson (right), governor and Democratic presidential candidate; Richard J. Daley (below), mayor of Chicago from 1955 until his death in 1976; Jane M. Byrne (far right, top), first woman mayor of Chicago; and Harold Washington (far right, bottom), first black mayor of Chicago.

chanted in unison, "The whole world is watching! The whole world is watching!"

Yet Daley's popularity with Chicago voters remained unshaken. He gave the people reliable city services such as street lighting that extended into the alleys and efficient garbage pick-up. Whatever people may have thought about his particular brand of machine politics, under his leadership Chicago was hailed as "the city that works."

Jane Byrne, Chicago's first woman mayor, served from 1979 to 1983. The city's first black mayor, Harold Washington, was elected in 1983. Washington's administration was clouded by constant skirmishes with the city council. Critics called the clash Council Wars after the popular *Star Wars* movies.

A debt crisis gripped Illinois farm country in the 1980s. After years of rising crop prices and dramatic increases in the value of farmland, many farmers borrowed large sums of money to expand their operations. Then, in the 1980s, crop prices tumbled and the value of farmland dropped radically. Farmers found themselves saddled with enormous debts and reduced means to repay their loans. Certainly this debt crisis was not a problem faced by Illinois farmers alone. It affected every farm state in the nation. Nevertheless, Illinois farmers grew bitter as the pounding of an auctioneer's hammer sold farms that had been in the same families for as long as a hundred years.

Another economic problem that worsened during the 1980s concerned the pockets of urban poverty in various parts of the state. These depressed areas had been deteriorating for more than twenty years. In many towns, industrial plants grew old or industry abandoned the area entirely. The southern Illinois town of East St. Louis serves as an example. Most of its residents are black. Fifty percent of the work force is unemployed, and two thirds of its people live on some form of public aid. Its streets are dotted with burned-out shells of houses and garbage-strewn lots. Most of its factory buildings stand vacant. Various plans to pump money into East St. Louis in order to begin rehabilitation have been proposed. But in the mid-1980s, the town was so poor that abandoned houses were not even worth the wrecker's fee needed to tear them down.

In recent times, the economy and the government's efforts to pull Illinois out of business and farm slumps have been the dominating factors in the state's affairs.

Chapter 7

GOVERNMENT AND THE ECONOMY

GOVERNMENT AND THE ECONOMY

If Illinois were a country, it would be one of the richest members of the United Nations. Every year, the state collects and spends more money and produces more goods than many of the world's independent countries.

GOVERNMENT

Like that of most other states, Illinois government is patterned after the federal government. It is divided into three branches: the legislative (lawmaking), executive (law-enforcing), and judicial (law-interpreting).

The state's legislative branch is called the General Assembly. It consists of a Senate with 59 senators and a House of Representatives with 118 state representatives. Senators are elected to terms of either two or four years. The terms are staggered so that the Senate cannot be completely overturned in a single election. Members of the House serve two-year terms. The General Assembly's job is to create new laws or to rescind or revise old ones. It also works with the governor to prepare the state budget.

The executive powers are held by the governor. The state governor is elected to a four-year term. The state constitution gives him the authority to veto or approve laws passed by the

General Assembly, to grant pardons, to serve as commander-in-chief of the state militia, and to call emergency sessions of the General Assembly.

The judicial branch interprets laws and tries cases. The Illinois court system consists of a supreme court, appellate courts, and circuit courts. The supreme court, the highest in the state, hears cases that are passed to it from the appellate and circuit courts. The Circuit Court of Cook County, with 140 judges, is the largest court in the United States.

TAXING AND SPENDING

Finances dominate political arguments in Illinois. The amount of money required to run the state is staggering. The state is Illinois' largest employer. More than one hundred thousand people work for the government. In the 1980s, the annual budget ranged between fifteen and seventeen billion dollars. During Abraham Lincoln's time, such a dollar figure would have been beyond comprehension.

Illinois' largest source of revenue is an income tax paid by every working citizen. Other sources of revenue are state sales and gasoline taxes, grants from the federal government, and a profitable lottery game. The average taxpayer in 1982 paid $1,197 to help run the state. Illinois spends most of its tax money on education. Public aid is another huge expense. Law enforcement and highway maintenance also comprise much of the state budget.

SCHOOLS

In the 1980s, the state spent $3.5 billion annually on its schools. Despite this large expenditure, however, additional money to

Buildings on the University of Chicago quadrangle

support school systems must come from city and township taxes. In 1983, there were 1.3 million grade-school students, and more than a half million secondary-school students. It costs the state about $3,000 per year to keep each student in school.

Private schools are important in the state's education system. About 15 percent of Illinois' school-age children attended non-public schools in the early 1980s. In Chicago, the Roman Catholic church runs the largest private-school system in the state.

Illinois has seventy-four major universities and colleges, counting both public and private institutions. The largest university is the state-supported University of Illinois at Champaign-Urbana. Its thirty-five thousand students represent every county in the state, every state in the Union, and about a hundred foreign nations. Founded in 1867, the University of Illinois has a history of service to the state, including being responsible for the introduction of soybeans to the Illinois farmer. The university has a major Chicago campus that serves twenty thousand students. Other large state-supported colleges are

The fertile prairie sod of Illinois continues to produce bountiful harvests.

Southern Illinois University at Carbondale and Northern Illinois University at DeKalb. Few universities in the United States are more highly regarded in academic circles than the University of Chicago. University of Chicago professors and students have won a host of Nobel Prizes, the crowning achievement of any scholar. In 1983, seven Nobel laureates were on the university's faculty, and fifty-three other Nobel Prize winners had taught or studied there in the past.

THE ECONOMY

Illinois is blessed with fertile land, plentiful natural resources, highly developed communications and transportation, and skilled workers. For these reasons it is a wealthy state. The average annual income of an Illinois worker in 1983 was $12,405. That is a higher annual wage than is earned in any other state in the Midwest.

Nevertheless, the Illinois economy was sluggish during the 1980s. Unemployment reached 9.2 percent in late 1984; that figure was two percentage points higher than the national average. In 1985, a Chicago business group claimed that the city had lost four hundred thousand jobs in the last decade. Sagging farm prices have put at least 20 percent of the state's farmers in financial difficulty. And nagging pockets of poverty such as the one in East St. Louis have created further financial problems.

The economic problems faced by Illinois are shared by other states in the heartland. The difficulties stem from competition from abroad, outdated equipment in some industrial plants, and declining prices for farm products. But even though some statistics appear to be grim, the state's assets and potential for progress far outweigh its current economic problems.

THE FARMS

The state's most outstanding resource is its rich black soil. The fertile prairie sod continues to produce bountiful harvests. Illinois leads all other states in the production of soybeans and alternates with Iowa in being the leading producer of corn. Other important crops include oats, wheat, barley, alfalfa, peaches, apples, and melons. Hogs are the chief meat animals raised in the state, followed by beef cattle and sheep. Dairy and poultry farming are important in the state's northern region.

The approximately 105,000 farms in Illinois cover 80 percent of the state. The average farm is 272 acres (110 hectares) in size, indicating that many family-owned farms still operate in Illinois. But it is the family farms that have been hit most severely by the debt crisis. Illinois' farm debts rose from $5.1 billion in 1977 to $11.3 billion in 1983—an increase of more than 100 percent in a six-year period. "People in the big cities don't realize what's going on out here [in southern Illinois]," the manager of a farm cooperative told a reporter during a 1985 interview. "It's common here for a farmer, and I mean a good farmer, not some guy who doesn't know what he's doing, to be $300,000 in debt, $400,000 in debt, even $500,000 in debt."

No one knows how the debt crisis will finally be resolved. Some observers of the farm scene grimly predict the end of the family farm as an institution. Farmers are a stoic lot, however, and are used to periods of hardship. So they wait and hope for good harvests and higher crop prices next year.

THE FACTORIES

Manufacturing provides about 1.2 million jobs for Illinois workers. Some eighteen thousand factories operate in the state, most of them in the Chicago area. Chicago factories produce household appliances, railroad and telephone equipment, automobiles, and a host of other items. The city's seventeen hundred printing firms produce everything from books to magazines, telephone directories to maps. Moline calls itself the "Farm Implement Capital of the World." Food processing is a combined $5 billion a year business for the cities of Decatur, Granite City, Pekin, and Summit. Candy, butter, and cheese are produced in various parts of the state.

Until the late 1970s, the Peoria-based Caterpillar Tractor Company, which produces huge bulldozers, had forty thousand workers and was the state's largest private employer. Today, however, the parking lots that surround Caterpillar plants are half-empty. Overseas companies now make the same bulldozers at a lower cost than Caterpillar is able to do. The fact that foreign workers are paid lower wages is only one reason for this development. Much of Caterpillar's factory equipment is obsolete, while foreign plants have become automated and are computerized. Journalists often call the ancient industrial complexes of Illinois and other midwestern states the "Rust Belt." Until these factories are modernized, many Illinois companies will limp along, as does Caterpillar, at 50 to 60 percent of their manufacturing capacity.

ENERGY AND NATURAL RESOURCES

As Saudi Arabia is to the world's oil supply, Illinois is to America's coal resources. Coal beds lie under two thirds of the state. Most of them are concentrated in the south. Illinois has a greater reserve of coal than any other state in the nation. The problem is that almost all of Illinois' deposits are bituminous (soft) coal with a high sulfur content. When burned, this coal spews pollutants into the air. Because of the danger of pollution, power companies and industries near large cities are not permitted to burn soft coal unless their smokestacks have scrubbers. Scientists, however, are devising methods of burning soft coal without releasing excess pollution. Some day, Illinois may be able to reap the full benefits from its enormous coal resources. The most promising recent development is the proposed construction of a synthetic fuel plant in Virden that would be able to use Illinois coal.

Illinois soil is also rich in other minerals. Lead and zinc can be found in the Galena area; natural gas in central Illinois; and clay, gravel, and limestone throughout the state. Silica sand, used to make glass, is abundant in southern Illinois. The glass-bottle manufacturing plants in Alton and Streator are among the largest such facilities in the world. Illinois also leads the nation in the mining of fluorspar, a mineral used in the steel and chemical industries.

Most Illinois electric plants burn coal to generate electricity. Often it is hard coal, which comes from out of state. A third of the state's power, however, is generated by nuclear plants. More nuclear plants are planned for the 1980s. Though Illinois was the birthplace of nuclear energy, many environmental groups fear the construction of more nuclear plants because of the possibility of a disastrous accident.

TRANSPORTATION AND COMMUNICATION

None of the state's farms, factories, or mines could function if they were not linked by railroads, highways, and airports. Illinois has some of the most advanced and extensive transportation facilities in the world. Railroads have been a major industry in the state since their beginning in the early 1800s. By 1900, the Illinois railroad industry boasted that no village in the state was more than fifteen miles (twenty-four kilometers) from some stretch of railroad track. Today, however, many miles of that track have been abandoned because trucking has become an important means of transporting freight. Illinois ranks second in the nation in the total number of interstate highway miles, enabling truck traffic to flow easily over the state.

Chicago's O'Hare Field is the world's busiest commercial airport. On an average day, two thousand planes land or take off there. Ninety-five other public airports are scattered over the state, but all are dwarfed by the tremendous activity at O'Hare.

Canals have been crucial to Chicago's history. In 1848, a shipping canal that linked the city with the Mississippi River

Left: A barge on the Chicago Sanitary and Ship Canal near Lockport
Below: Chicago's O'Hare Field, the busiest commercial airport in the world

system was completed. The Chicago Sanitary and Ship Canal, dug in the 1890s, helped complete the engineering miracle that reversed the flow of the Chicago River so that sewage would no longer flow into Lake Michigan. Chicago became an international shipping port in 1959 when the Great Lakes were connected to the Atlantic Ocean by the St. Lawrence Seaway.

Illinois has 720 newspapers, 300 radio stations, and 30 television stations. Johnson Publications, the largest black-owned firm in the nation, is based in Chicago. It produces *Ebony, Jet, EM,* and *Ebony Jr.* magazines. Until the late 1970s, Chicago had four major daily papers. Today it has only two—the *Chicago Tribune* and the *Chicago Sun-Times.* Other major dailies in the state include the *Springfield State Journal-Register,* the *Alton Telegraph,* the *Rockford Register-Star,* and the *Joliet Herald-News.*

Chapter 8
WORKS THAT LIVE

WORKS THAT LIVE

A building will stand for generations after its designer dies. Likewise, a great book will be read for centuries. In Illinois history, many men and women have achieved a certain degree of immortality through their imposing buildings or their written words. The genius of its architects and writers has enriched the cultural heritage of Illinois.

ARCHITECTURE

When the Chicago Fire of 1871 left the city in ruins, the colossal job of rebuilding led to an architectural renaissance. Talented architects such as William Le Baron Jenney, Daniel H. Burnham, and Louis Sullivan came to Chicago, excited by the opportunity to rebuild a major city from the ground up. These architects created the Chicago school of architecture.

Chicago-school architects used the most advanced structural materials in their buildings. As a result, the airiness of glass-covered steel beams replaced the bulk of stone walls. The Carson Pirie Scott Building, designed by Louis Sullivan and built in the 1890s, still stands as a monument to the Chicago school. Students of architecture come from all over the world to marvel at the building's ornate ironwork and the revolutionary openness of its design.

The Carson Pirie Scott Building (left), designed by Louis Sullivan and built in the 1890s, stands as a monument to the Chicago school of architecture. Second-generation Chicago-school architect Ludwig Mies van der Rohe designed the Illinois Institute of Technology's Crown Hall (above).

The Chicago school's greatest contribution to world architecture was the skyscraper. The first true skyscraper, designed by the founder of the Chicago school, William Le Baron Jenney, was completed in 1885. The ten-story Home Insurance Building rose on a skeleton of cast-iron and steel beams and had lightweight walls that hung like curtains to its frame. All high-rise buildings erected since have been based on the same construction formula.

German-American architect Ludwig Mies van der Rohe began a second-generation Chicago school in the 1940s. His Lake Shore Drive apartment buildings are masterpieces of glass and steel. However, his works remain the subject of endless arguments among Chicagoans. Mies's admirers hail his buildings as being "clean" in design. His critics condemn them as being "antiseptic."

Architect Helmut Jahn designed the striking State of Illinois Building in downtown Chicago (above). Chicago's John Hancock Building (right) is one of the world's tallest skyscrapers.

Chicagoans have an almost affectionate attitude toward the forest of office buildings towering above their downtown Loop. They have given nicknames to large buildings—"Big John" for the John Hancock Building and "Big Stan" for the Standard Oil Building, for instance. Four of the world's ten tallest buildings are located in downtown Chicago. The giant of them all is Sears Tower, which is even taller than New York's World Trade Center. And that's a fact Chicagoans are likely to boast about.

In home design, few architects have been able to rival Frank Lloyd Wright. Wright, who is considered one of the most important architects of the twentieth century, spent his most productive years building homes in the Chicago area. He believed

Frank Lloyd Wright, one of the most important architects of the twentieth century, designed "prairie-style" houses such as Robie House (above) with low, horizontal shapes that merged gracefully with the flat Illinois landscape.

that houses should conform to their surroundings. So his Illinois houses were built in the "prairie style" with low, horizontal shapes that merged gracefully with the flat landscape. Low-slung Robie House, built in 1909 and now owned by the University of Chicago, is an excellent example of the prairie style. Many other fascinating Wright-designed houses can be seen in Oak Park and other Chicago suburbs.

One of the brightest Chicago architects of the 1980s is German-born Helmut Jahn. He specializes in huge projects that include towering high-rise buildings. Working for Chicago-based firms, he was influenced by the unadorned glass and steel structures of Ludwig Mies van der Rohe, but Jahn's work took a brave new course with his striking State of Illinois Building in downtown Chicago. The *Chicago Tribune* described it as "the most visually startling building in the Loop since the first skyscraper went up."

LITERATURE

Illinois has produced many renowned writers and poets. In the early 1900s, a group of writers took their readers into the back streets of the city slums and the midsts of sweatshop factories. They were labeled muckrakers by President Theodore Roosevelt, who accused the group of forever turning up filth. Frank Norris and Upton Sinclair were famous Illinois muckrakers. Sinclair's 1906 novel *The Jungle* told the story of brutal working conditions in the Chicago stockyards and alarmed readers by exposing the rat-infested, filthy slaughterhouses where meat was processed. Public outcry generated by the book helped to goad Congress into passing the Pure Food and Drug Act.

While the muckrakers stirred the nation's conscience, a young visionary named Vachel Lindsay began writing poetry. Born in Springfield in 1879, Lindsay would have been labeled a "beatnik" or "hippie" poet had he lived in a later era. He wandered about the country reading his verses in exchange for food and shelter. A dedicated vagabond who rejected middle-class comforts, Lindsay once wrote in his diary, "If I cannot beat the system I can die protesting." Some of his best-known poems include "The Eagle that Is Forgotten" (1913) and "Abraham Lincoln Walks at Midnight" (1914).

Encouraging Lindsay and other poets was Chicagoan Harriet Monroe, the driving force behind a magazine with the simple title *Poetry: A Magazine of Verse.* In *Poetry,* Monroe published the works of young and revolutionary poets who were routinely rejected by the established magazines. She helped launch the "Chicago Renaissance," an exciting period of literary creativity that lasted from 1912 to 1930.

Poets Edgar Lee Masters and Carl Sandburg were keystones in

the Chicago Renaissance, and were often published in *Poetry* magazine. Edgar Lee Masters lived in Lewistown, Illinois, near the Spoon River. In 1915, he wrote a collection of mystical poems called *Spoon River Anthology.* Each poem gives a voice to a dead soul residing in the Spoon River cemetery. Carl Sandburg, who was born in Galesburg, became renowned for his poetry, his biography of Lincoln, his knowledge of folk songs, and his books for children. His best-known poem, written in 1916, celebrates his adopted city, Chicago:

> Hog Butcher for the World,
> Tool Maker, Stacker of Wheat,
> Player with Railroads and the Nation's Freight Handler;
> Stormy, husky, brawling,
> City of the Broad Shoulders.

Ernest Hemingway, one of the most influential writers of the twentieth century, was born in Oak Park, a western suburb of Chicago. Two of his 1920s novels—*The Sun Also Rises* and *A Farewell to Arms*—concerned the "Lost Generation" of Americans who fought in World War I. Hemingway spent most of his life outside of his native state. A colorful man, he enjoyed hunting big game in Africa, carousing in European cities, and relaxing on the beaches of Cuba.

Important Illinois writers of the 1920s and 1930s include Sherwood Anderson, John Dos Passos, and James T. Farrell. Sherwood Anderson was born and grew up in Ohio. While in his thirties, he deserted his family, quit his job, and moved to Chicago to write. His collection of short stories called *Winesburg, Ohio* denounced what he saw as the narrowness of midwestern American life. John Dos Passos, like Hemingway, was disillusioned by the post-World War I world. His trilogy *U.S.A.*

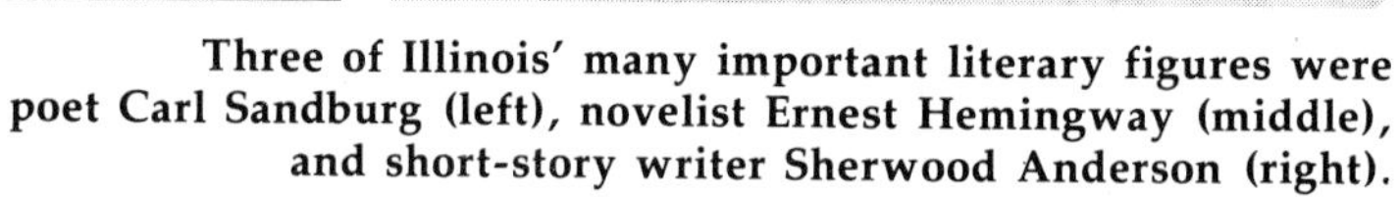

Three of Illinois' many important literary figures were poet Carl Sandburg (left), novelist Ernest Hemingway (middle), and short-story writer Sherwood Anderson (right).

opens in Chicago, the city of his birth. James T. Farrell's most popular work was the *Studs Lonigan* trilogy—three books based on the life of a young tough who grew up fighting for existence on Chicago's South Side. Its gruff style both shocked and delighted readers of the 1930s.

After World War II, an exciting new generation of writers who portrayed life with biting realism lived and worked in Chicago.

Nelson Algren wrote stories and novels about the shot-and-beer workingman's neighborhood where he lived. Black novelist Willard Motley wrote powerful books about the down-and-outers and the outright crooks who inhabited the West Side slums. Gwendolyn Brooks, poet laureate of Illinois, was an angry black writer in the days when such a stance took considerable courage. Her poem "Negro Hero" begins:

> I had to kick their law into their teeth in order to save them.
> However, I have heard that sometimes you have to deal
> Devilishly with drowning men in order to swim them to shore.

Illinois-born novelist James Jones received lasting fame for his World War II book *From Here to Eternity.* It was Jones's first novel, and at the time of its publication was considered the best book to come out of the war. University of Chicago professor and novelist Saul Bellow won the Nobel Prize in literature in 1976. His novels are set in various parts of the world, but he is particularly vivid when describing Chicago, the city where he grew up.

Journalists and nonfiction writers command Chicago's literary scene today. Author Studs Terkel collects American oral history. His World War II collection, *The Good War,* won the Pulitzer Prize in 1984. The city's most popular, and often most controversial, journalist is Mike Royko, whose daily newspaper column is syndicated throughout the country. His book *Boss* told of political corruption during Mayor Daley's era. In his column, Royko sometimes spins yarns about a fictional boyhood friend named Slats Grobnik who grew up in "a second-floor flat above a tavern with the L tracks in the back." What kind of boy was he? Royko tells of Slats's father warning him to stay out of trouble with the police: " 'Just one arrest, kid, and you'll never get no job.' Slats answered: 'That won't interfere with my plans.' "

Chapter 9
SPORTS AND LEISURE

SPORTS AND LEISURE

Like most Americans, Illinois residents are hard workers, but everyone enjoys an occasional day off. Sports and outdoor activities, music, and theatergoing are some of the activities that occupy the leisure time of Illinois residents.

SPORTS

For professional sports entertainment, Illinois fans tend to follow the exploits of Chicago teams. In the last forty years, however, Chicago's professional athletes have had a frustrating tradition of near greatness and utter failure.

In football, the Chicago Bears of the 1930s and '40s were a feared team nicknamed the Monsters of the Midway; but until recently, they could be called the Munchkins of the Midway. Only the feats of two exceptional running backs—Gale Sayers in the 1960s and Walter Payton in the 1970s and '80s—kept the team interesting. But in 1985, under coach Mike Ditka, the Bears finally fielded a team reminiscent of the Midway Monsters of old. Ditka, running back Walter Payton, and a savage defense led the Bears to a 15-1 regular season. The team crushed their opponents in the playoffs and devastated the New England Patriots in Super Bowl XX at New Orleans. Football experts called the 1985-86 Bears one of the greatest teams ever.

The Chicago Cubs play baseball in the "friendly confines" of beautiful Wrigley Field, with its old-fashioned manual scoreboard, ivy-covered outfield wall, and the city skyline as a backdrop.

Professional baseball in Chicago is a friendly civil war. The White Sox play on the South Side and the Cubs on the North Side. Early on, Illinois fans have to make the difficult choice of devoting their loyalties to either one or the other. Once a fan chooses his team, there can be no switching. Tradition forbids such wishy-washy behavior. Though the White Sox have had slightly greater success than the Cubs over the past forty years, the Cubs command a fanatical following that is the envy of almost every franchise in the Major Leagues.

The Cubs. No sports team in history has set such a long-standing record of futility. They have not won a pennant since 1945, prompting cynics to declare, "The last time the Cubs won, Japan lost." They have employed, among other players, an outfielder who, when criticized about his fielding ability, answered, "Awww, I only have trouble with fly balls," and a rookie who was leading the league in hitting until he told a television interviewer, "Sure, I have a weakness; I can't hit an inside curve ball."

Despite laughable ballplayers who have been fielded over the years, the sunny bleachers and grandstands of Wrigley Field, home of the Cubs, remain a Mecca for baseball fans. For generations, the ball park was the only stadium in the Major Leagues without lights. Finally—with an incredible amount of fanfare—the Cubs' owners installed lights at Wrigley Field and the team played its first night game there on August 8, 1988.

The Chicago Bulls of the National Basketball Association (NBA) are led by Michael Jordan, considered by many to be the finest all-around player of the 1980s. "Air" Jordan seems to defy gravity with his daring and graceful leaps to the basket. In the 1960s, Chicago's professional hockey team, the Blackhawks, fielded a powerful squad headed by such stars as Stan Mikita and Bobby Hull.

High-school basketball is the most popular amateur sport followed in the state. Illinois fans, like many midwesterners, support their state's high-school championship playoffs with unbridled passion. Basketball is often thought of as a city game, but in Illinois it is played with intensity both on inner-city playgrounds and in rural gyms. College basketball at De Paul University is followed closely by most Chicagoans. De Paul's coach Ray Meyer led the team for forty years before his retirement in 1984. Coach Meyer remains one of the most popular sports figures in the Chicago area.

College football fails to generate the fanatical loyalty it enjoys in other states. Illinois regionalism might be part of the reason for this. The University of Illinois team plays in Champaign-Urbana, far from the huge number of sports fans in Chicago. The nearest major college football team to Chicago is the Northwestern Wildcats, who play in suburban Evanston. Northwestern is respected for its devotion to scholarship, but other teams in the rugged Big Ten Conference consider playing the Wildcats the same as having a day off.

Fishing and horseback riding are among the many outdoor sports enjoyed by Illinois residents and visitors alike.

OUTDOOR RECREATION

Tourism is a big business in the state. Every year vacationers spend $4 billion in Illinois. Most of the tourists are family groups who enjoy outdoor activities, and in Illinois they are rarely disappointed. Illinois has seventy-two state parks, thirty-nine conservation areas, four state forests, and one national forest. Hiking, backpacking, and horseback riding are popular in these park facilities. A pamphlet issued by the state Tourist Department claims that Illinois, with its five hundred rivers and streams, has 2,000 miles (3,218 kilometers) of navigable canoe routes.

Many Illinois state parks and recreation areas lie in its scenic river valleys. White Pines State Park winds along the Fox River valley; for generations it has served as a campground for Chicago-area Boy Scouts and Girl Scouts. Starved Rock State Park, on the

Illinois River, is both a scenic wonderland and an important site in Illinois history.

Lakes and rivers in southern Illinois abound with crappie, catfish, white bass, bluegill, and walleye. A state-record bluegill, weighing five pounds (two kilograms) recently was pulled from the waters of Rend Lake.

Hunting is carefully controlled in Illinois. This is necessary largely because of the slaughter committed by the pioneers. The early settlers found the prairies alive with buffalo, elk, bears, and even mountain lions. But they shot all animals that came within rifle range. By the early 1800s, most of the exotic wildlife had vanished from within Illinois' boundaries. Even deer, which once roamed the prairie by the thousands, were virtually extinct by 1910. Then, in the 1930s, the Department of Conservation reintroduced deer to Illinois forests. Due to strict control over hunting, the deer herds thrive today.

PERFORMING ARTS

"Music is the universal language of mankind," said American poet Henry Wadsworth Longfellow. In Illinois, every imaginable type of this universal language is spoken. Go to southern Illinois for country music. Go to northern Illinois for the latest in rock. And don't forget Chicago, whose symphony orchestra commands the respect of the world.

Jazz, that uniquely American form of music, came to Illinois in the 1920s, when the gifted black horn player Louis "Satchmo" Armstrong moved to Chicago from his native New Orleans. A group of young white Chicago musicians became caught up in the captivating beat of the music that Armstrong and other blacks had brought up from the South. Adapting the new musical form to their own tastes, they began to play what came to be called Chicago-style jazz. In the 1930s, Chicago-born musical prodigy Benny Goodman took jazz into the "swing era" and made his music popular throughout the nation. Benny Goodman's was the first major band to include both black and white musicians.

The Chicago Symphony Orchestra, under the baton of Sir Georg Solti, is perhaps the world's finest classical orchestra. If anything, the orchestra may be a victim of its own success. Concertgoers complain that they must order symphony tickets a year in advance to be sure of getting seats. On a summer evening, however, lovers of classical music need only travel to Grant Park on the lakeshore and sit on the grass to listen to the Grant Park Symphony. Since 1935, the Grant Park orchestra has given free concerts to the public. Another popular outdoor summer music festival is held at Ravinia in suburban Highland Park.

The Chicago City Ballet, established in 1980, is already a popular classical-dance attraction. The company tours central and southern Illinois and plays in other midwestern cities. Smaller dance groups such as the Joseph Holmes Dance Theater and the MoMing Dance and Arts Center experiment with new music and dance techniques.

Plays and musicals imported from Broadway and elsewhere are presented at a number of downtown Chicago theaters, including the Shubert, the Blackstone, the Auditorium, and the Arie Crown. It is the recent appearance of a number of "off-Loop" theaters and repertory companies, however, that has made Chicago one of the most exciting centers for theater in America. In the early 1970s, young theater producers began to lease empty factory buildings that dotted some North Side neighborhoods. Rows of seats and stages were hammered together, and a new Chicago theater tradition was born.

Sir Georg Solti is the conductor of the Chicago Symphony Orchestra, perhaps the world's finest classical orchestra.

The award-winning Steppenwolf Theatre company performs in one of these converted factory buildings. Steppenwolf produces classic plays, new plays, old plays, and previously rejected plays. A nearby gray brick building houses the Victory Garden Theater, where at least four new plays a year are performed, many of them written by unknown Chicago playwrights. Other small theater groups scattered over the North Side include Body Politic, The Organic Theatre Company, and Remains.

Two of Chicago's older, established theater companies are Goodman and Second City. The Goodman Theater building is a 683-seat Gothic masterpiece located behind the famous Art Institute of Chicago. For more than fifty years, Goodman has served Chicago theatergoers. An especially popular children's show is its annual performance of *A Christmas Carol.*

Chicago also has a long tradition of improvisational theater. Second City Theatre, which has been presenting improvisation-based revues for twenty-five years, was the first group of its kind, and has launched the careers of many famous actors and actresses.

Harrison
HOTEL
PARK FREE
TORCO

Chapter 10

HIGHLIGHTS OF THE PRAIRIE STATE

HIGHLIGHTS OF THE PRAIRIE STATE

Everyone complains that vacations are always too short. Take, for example, a two-week trip through Illinois. How does one determine where to stop and what to skip? Driving from north to south, a quick tour through the state might include the following stops.

THE CHICAGO LAKEFRONT

No cityscape in the world can rival Chicago's lakefront area. A long strip of land hugging Chicago's sparkling lakeshore, it is crammed with beaches, grassy parks, and museums. To the credit of the city's early planners, almost the entire shore along Lake Michigan is devoted to public parkland.

Buckingham Fountain is the centerpiece of Grant Park, located between Chicago's lakeshore and the downtown Loop area (so-called because the L tracks circle or "loop" around it). On summer nights, blazing colored lights dance on jets of water that shoot up from the marvelous fountain. Chicagoans and visitors alike enjoy listening to a free concert at the park and then watching the last light display of the evening. Grant Park is the site of four popular museums. The Art Institute of Chicago houses one of the world's finest collections of paintings and sculptures. The Adler Planetarium dazzles visitors with its presentations of the heavens.

The centerpiece of Chicago's Grant Park (below) is Buckingham Fountain (left), which displays a dazzling light show on summer nights. The Art Institute (above) is especially famous for its fine collection of French Impressionist paintings.

Lake Shore Drive (right) is a broad thoroughfare that runs along the lakefront from the far north side of the city to the far south side and connects Chicago's three major lakefront parks.

At the Shedd Aquarium, brilliantly colored fish from all over the world flash about their tanks. Dinosaur bones, Egyptian mummies, and other relics of the past are housed in the Field Museum of Natural History.

South of the Loop, Jackson Park stretches over 543 acres (220 hectares) along the lakefront. Jackson Park is the home of the Museum of Science and Industry, where glass-enclosed spinning gears and pumping pistons help to illustrate the history of machinery. Also featured are a captured German submarine and a replica of an operating coal mine. Near Jackson Park is the Du Sable Museum of African American History. Named after Chicago's first citizen, it contains exhibits of the contributions of black people to American society.

The Lincoln Park area, north of the Loop, is one of the most prestigious neighborhoods in Chicago. Gleaming high-rise buildings tower above its tree-lined sidewalks. Rents there are among the highest in the city. The park is the home of a glass-enclosed conservatory, the world-famous Lincoln Park Zoo, and

Beautiful Lincoln Park is a magnet for North Side residents, who use it year round for a variety of outdoor activities.

the Chicago Historical Society museum. The park also serves as the outdoor gymnasium for the North Side. Its golf course, beaches, bicycle lanes, jogging tracks, and tennis courts are always alive with people.

The three lakefront parks are connected by a broad thoroughfare called Lake Shore Drive. Running parallel to "The Drive" is North Michigan Avenue. Here Chicago's smartest shops are located. The stretch of shops along this boulevard is often called the "Magnificent Mile." The lively Rush Street area, heart of the city's nightlife, is nearby. Farther north along the lakefront rise the graceful mansions built around the turn of the nineteenth century in such suburbs as Wilmette, Glencoe, and Lake Forest.

ROCKFORD TO GALENA

Rockford is about a two-hour drive due west from Chicago. Before any settlement existed there, stagecoaches on the Chicago-to-Galena line used to cross the Rock River at a shallow, stone-bottomed ford. Hence the name Rockford. The Rock River still

The historic town of Galena on the Mississippi River attracts a large number of visitors, most of whom arrive especially to take the annual tours of the town's beautifully restored Victorian homes.

flows through the center of this town, which is now the state's second-largest city. A fine public library in the heart of downtown, lavish homes along the riverfront, and several small but interesting museums are located in Rockford.

On the westward road from Rockford to Galena, flat cornfields give way to rugged hill country. Along the way, one can drive through scenic, forested Apple River Canyon State Park, where the tiny Apple River twists and bends to carve a series of stark and beautiful canyons out of a bed of limestone.

History comes alive in the town of Galena on the Mississippi River. In 1850, Galena was the most promising community in northern Illinois, and many people believed it would eventually eclipse Chicago. Galena's importance faded after the Civil War, however, and it became a backwater village. But today's visitors are delighted to find that the houses of its halcyon days still stand, like decorative monuments to a bygone era. Many of the homes that dot the bluffs have been carefully restored by their proud owners. Prominent among the houses is one that belonged to

Ottawa Canyon in Starved Rock State Park

Ulysses S. Grant, eighteenth president of the United States. The city gave the house to General Grant when he returned to his hometown as a Civil War hero.

South of Galena, a scenic highway hugs the Mississippi River and cuts through Mississippi Palisades State Park. The ride along the riverbank is one of the prettiest drives in the state. Hiking trails inside the park twist along wind-swept bluffs that offer striking views of the broad Mississippi.

CENTRAL ILLINOIS

Starved Rock State Park (about a two-hour drive from Chicago), with its marvelous scenery, is steeped in Illinois history. In the center of the park stands the huge rock formation that rises 140 feet (43 meters) above the Illinois River. Marquette and Jolliet visited the site and La Salle established a fort on the summit of the rock. Starved Rock was named during the Indian wars that raged during the 1700s. One tribe tried to escape its enemies by climbing to the rock's broad, flat top, but found itself encircled and was starved into submission. Today, a wooden staircase takes visitors to the high bluff that commands a spectacular view of the gently

Starved Rock, the huge rock formation that rises above the Illinois River

flowing Illinois River. Were it not for the dam near the rock, the riverbank would look much as it did in La Salle's time.

In the central Illinois town of Galesburg, visitors can tour the boyhood home of famous Illinois poet Carl Sandburg. When Sandburg died in 1967, his ashes were buried under a nearby boulder called Remembrance Rock, the name of one of Sandburg's books.

Also in central Illinois is Lewistown, the home of Edgar Lee Masters, another of the state's renowned poets. Lewistown is the heart of Masters's "Spoon River Country," where sluggish rivers flow through quiet towns.

The sprawling city of Peoria, the unofficial capital of central Illinois, is the third-largest city in the state. The pride of the city's downtown area is the newly completed Civic Center. The self-contained twenty-acre (eight-hectare) complex is the state's largest convention center outside Chicago. Peoria is also proud of its forty-four neighborhood parks.

Peoria was founded three hundred years ago by French explorer Sieur de La Salle. It was the first permanent European settlement on the mid-American continent. In the early 1800s, Peoria was a steamboat port for the booming Illinois River trade. Today, its only remaining steamboat takes visitors on tours of the river country.

South of Peoria lies Pekin, the birthplace of Illinois Senator

Everett Dirksen. Senator Dirksen, who died in 1969, was once an amateur actor who enjoyed playing Shakespearean roles. His speaking voice, according to one writer, was "now a whisper, now a deep growl, now rolling thunder."

North of Peoria is Tampico, where another actor-turned-politician was born. President Ronald Reagan grew up in central Illinois, and as a young man worked as a radio sportscaster, bringing play-by-play descriptions of Chicago Cub games to listeners in the region.

SPRINGFIELD AND NEW SALEM VILLAGE

Springfield, the state capital, was the home of Illinois' most prominent citizen. The only home that Abraham Lincoln ever owned is just a short walk from downtown Springfield. The comfortable, two-story frame house has been restored to look as it did in Lincoln's time. Knowledgeable tour guides point out details such as the crystal bowl holding pieces of rock candy, a treat enjoyed by the Lincoln children. Nearby houses, many of which were owned by Lincoln's friends, also have been preserved. A stroll through the neighborhood is like a century-long step back into time.

The Old State Capitol Building in the middle of downtown Springfield now serves as a museum of state government. Lincoln was a daily visitor to this dome-capped building when he was a young lawyer. The present Capitol Building was first occupied by the General Assembly in 1876. Inside the building are murals depicting scenes of Illinois history, and portraits and statues of former dignitaries. The nearby Illinois State Museum has outstanding displays of Indian life in Illinois before the arrival of white settlers.

The restored log-cabin settlement of New Salem Village gives visitors a view of Illinois pioneer life.

The restored log-cabin settlement of New Salem Village is a twenty-minute drive from downtown Springfield. Abraham Lincoln was a young man in 1831 when he literally ran into New Salem Village. A riverboat he was working on became stuck in the mud near this cluster of cabins. Lincoln decided to stay, and got a job as a clerk in a general store. The village people liked the tall, lanky young man, and chose him to be their postmaster. It was the first public office Lincoln ever held. After the settlers abandoned the village in the 1850s, their log cabins gradually fell to pieces. But the reconstructed town gives visitors a splendid idea of pioneer life in Illinois.

It is said that Lincoln often walked the fifteen miles (twenty-four kilometers) or more from New Salem Village to Springfield in order to borrow books. Today, Boy Scouts on weekend trips who take the same hike complain that the trek is exhausting.

SOUTHERN ILLINOIS

Cahokia Mounds State Park near East St. Louis was once hallowed ground that belonged to the state's Indians. Early white settlers refused to plant crops on the mysterious mounds because they feared the wrath of some long-ago Indian god. Later studies confirmed that the mounds were Indian burial sites. One of them,

Monk's Mound, is the largest prehistoric earthwork in the world.

The flat prairie land breaks into gentle hills on the approach to Shawnee National Forest. This sprawling wooded area spreads over 260,000 acres (105,222 hectares) of spectacular countryside. A road cuts through a magnificent river valley called the Garden of the Gods. At Crab Orchard Lake, more than half a million Canada geese find winter quarters. Because much of this national forest is inaccessible by automobile, only hardy canoers and backpackers can enter its interior and behold its undisturbed wonders.

Shawneetown is an old settlement on the banks of the Ohio River. A story persists that in the pioneer era, Shawneetown's most prominant banker refused to grant a loan to a northern village because he believed the place was simply an isolated cluster of houses that had no possibility of growth. The name of that northern village was Chicago.

The river delta city of Cairo is the southernmost city of Illinois. It was a boom town during the Civil War when the *Cairo Gazette* reported that "Every house, cellar, and shed is occupied as a place of business and every occupant is doing well." Mark Twain immortalized Cairo when he made it the destination of Huck and his friend Jim in the classic novel *Huckleberry Finn.* Today, Cairo is a lumber-processing town with an imposing collection of Victorian homes, many of which have been carefully restored.

Illinois men and women from Chicago to Cairo believe theirs is the most American of all the states. The nation's ills are their ills, and the hopes of America burn in their hearts. "How will it play in Peoria?" remains a valid question because the challenges faced by the state are identical to those the nation as a whole must confront. And Americans and Illinoisans together have always risen to whatever task looms ahead of them.

NATIONAL UNION
STATE
1868
1818
ILLINOIS

FACTS AT A GLANCE

GENERAL INFORMATION

Statehood: December 3, 1818, twenty-first state

Origin of Name: French form of the word *Illiniwek,* the name of a group of Indians who lived in Illinois prior to the arrival of white settlers; *Illiniwek* means "the men" or "the superior men"

State Capital: Springfield, founded 1821

State Nickname: "Land of Lincoln" official state nickname; also called the "Prairie State"

State Flag: Illinois has had two official state flags. The first, adopted in 1915, shows a replica of the state seal. An eagle holding a red banner in its beak is pictured against a white background. The state motto is written on the banner. The eagle also holds a shield with thirteen stars and stripes symbolizing the original thirteen states. An olive branch below the shield stands for peace, and a sun rising over plains in the background stands for the Illinois prairie. The eagle stands on a rock that bears two dates—1818, the year Illinois was admitted to the union, and 1868, the year the state seal was adopted. In 1969, Chief Petty Officer Bruce McDaniel, an American soldier serving in Vietnam, requested that the state's name be added to the flag. He had noticed that no one could identify Illinois' flag among the many other state flags hanging on the wall of his mess hall. In 1970, his request was approved and a new official state flag, carrying the old image but with the name "Illinois" added, was adopted.

State Motto: "State Sovereignty, National Union"

State Bird: Cardinal

State Animal: White-tailed deer

State Fish: Bluegill

State Flower: Native violet

State Tree: White oak

State Insect: Monarch butterfly

State Mineral: Fluorite

State Song: "Illinois," words by Charles H. Chamberlain, sung to the tune "Baby Mine"; adopted as the official state song in 1925:

By thy rivers gently flowing, Illinois, Illinois,
O'er thy prairies verdant growing, Illinois, Illinois,
Comes an echo on the breeze,
Rustling through the leafy trees, and its mellow tones are these,
Illinois, Illinois,
And its mellow tones are these, Illinois.

From a wilderness of prairies, Illinois, Illinois,
Straight thy way and never varies, Illinois, Illinois,
Till upon the inland sea,
Stands thy great commercial tree, turning all the world to thee,
Illinois, Illinois,
Turning all the world to thee, Illinois.

When you heard your country calling, Illinois, Illinois,
Where the shot and shell were falling, Illinois, Illinois,
When the Southern host withdrew,
Pitting Gray against the Blue, there were none more brave than you,
Illinois, Illinois,
There were none more brave than you, Illinois.

Not without thy wondrous story, Illinois, Illinois,
Can be writ the nation's glory, Illinois, Illinois,
On the record of thy years,
Abraham Lincoln's name appears, Grant and Logan, and our tears,
Illinois, Illinois,
Grant and Logan and our tears, Illinois.

POPULATION

Population: 11,427,414 (1980 census), sixth among the states (1987 estimate)

Population Density: 202.6 people per sq. mi. (78.2 people per km²)

Population Distribution: 83 percent of the people live in cities or towns. More than 60 percent live in the Chicago metropolitan area.

City	Population
Chicago	3,005,072
Rockford	139,712
Peoria	124,160
Springfield	99,637
Decatur	94,081
Aurora	81,293
Joliet	77,956
Evanston	73,706
Waukegan	67,653

(Population figures according to 1980 census)

Population Growth: Illinois' population expanded tremendously during its pioneer era, but in recent years its population growth has tapered off compared to that of the country as a whole. From 1970 to 1980, the state's population grew 2.8 percent, while the population of the entire country grew 11.45 percent. The list below shows population growth in Illinois since 1820:

Year	Population
1820	55,211
1840	476,183
1860	1,711,951
1880	3,077,871
1900	4,821,550
1920	6,485,280
1940	7,897,241
1950	8,712,176
1960	10,081,158
1970	11,113,976
1980	11,427,414

GEOGRAPHY

Borders: States that border Illinois are Wisconsin on the north, Indiana on the east, Kentucky on the south, and Missouri and Iowa on the west.

Highest Point: Charles Mound, 1,235 ft. (376 m)

Lowest Point: On the Mississippi River in Alexander County, 279 ft. (85 m)

Greatest Distances: North to south—385 mi. (620 km)
East to west—218 mi. (351 km)

Area: 56,400 sq. mi. (146,082 km^2)

Rank in Area Among the States: Twenty-fourth

Rivers: The more than five hundred rivers and streams that flow through Illinois provide the state with an extensive drainage system. The Mississippi River, which flows through the state for 518 mi. (833 km), is the longest river in Illinois. It forms the entire western border of the state. Lake Michigan is linked to the Mississippi River by the Illinois Waterway, which includes the Chicago, Des Plaines, and Illinois rivers. The Illinois River, 273 mi. (439 km) long, is the largest river lying wholly within the state. The Chicago River once flowed eastward into Lake Michigan, but has been reversed by a series of locks to flow west into the Des Plaines River. The Wabash River forms the southeastern border of Illinois. Though the Ohio River determines the state's southern border, the river itself is entirely in Kentucky; Kentucky's border runs along the north shore of the river. Other major rivers in Illinois are the Rock, Vermilion, Fox, Sangamon, Spoon, Kankakee, Embarras, Big Muddy, Kaskaskia, Pecatonica, Calumet, and Kishwaukee.

The Mississippi River as seen from Mississippi Palisades State Park

Lakes: A 63 mi. (101 km) stretch of Lake Michigan shoreline forms the northeast border of Illinois. Many artificial lakes have been created to make up for the relatively small number of natural lakes lying within the state. In all, there are about 950 lakes and reservoirs, covering a total of 282,000 acres (114,125 hectares) not including Lake Michigan. Man-made Lake Carlyle, covering 26,000 acres (10,522 hectares), is the largest lake lying wholly within the state. Crab Orchard Lake and Rend Lake are other large artificial lakes. Chain O'Lakes is a summer resort area in northeastern Illinois comprising a string of ten natural lakes. Other lakes in Illinois are Goose, Peoria, Senachwine, Springfield, Decatur, Bloomington, Lake of Egypt, and Lake Shelbyville.

Topography: The predominately flat land of Illinois is a result of glacier movements that occurred thousands of years ago. The state can be divided into three topographic regions—the Central Plains, the Shawnee Hills, and the Gulf Coastal Plain.

The Central Plains, which cover 90 percent of the state, can be divided into three areas. The Great Lakes Plain, which was once covered by Lake Michigan, is a level area of fertile soil situated in the northeast corner of the state. Chicago is included in this area. To the north and west of Chicago, the flatlands give way to hills, marshes, small lakes, and ravines. The wide, flat plains of fertile soil that cover the entire central part of the state are called the Till Plains. This area, sometimes called the "Garden Spot of the Nation," is Illinois' chief farming section. Because the Driftless Area, in the northwest corner of the state, was not touched by glaciers, it has the state's highest hills and deepest valleys. Illinois' highest point, Charles Mound, is found here.

The Shawnee Hills are a band of valleys, forested hills, woods, and river bluffs that spread for 70 mi. (113 km) across the southern part of the state. This land, which ranges from 300 to 1,065 ft. (91 to 325 m) high, is sometimes called the Illinois Ozarks.

The southernmost tip of Illinois is called the Gulf Coastal Plain. It is the northern end of a plain that stretches all the way to the Gulf of Mexico. Although the northern part of this region is hilly, the southern part is flat.

Climate: Illinois' climate varies greatly not only from season to season, but from day to day. Warm or cold winds can sweep into the state from any direction because there are no mountains to block them. As a result, the temperature can change as much as 20° F. (11° C) in one hour. Northern Illinois generally has harsher winters and cooler summers than southern Illinois. The average temperature in January is 25° F. (-4° C) in the north and 36° F. (2° C) in the south. The average temperature in July is 75° F. (24° C) in northern Illinois and 79° F. (26° C) in southern Illinois. Although the north receives heavier snowfall, the average amount of precipitation, including rainfall, snow, and other moisture, is greater in the south. The highest recorded temperature in Illinois was 117° F. (47°C) at East St. Louis on July 14, 1954. The lowest temperature on record was -35° F. (-37° C) at Mount Carroll on January 22, 1930.

NATURE

Trees: Oak, white oak, hickory, walnut, hard maple, sycamore, elm, tamarack, bald cypress, tupelo gum

Wild Plants: More than 2,400 kinds of wild plants grow in Illinois, including chess, wild barley, gumweed, bloodroot, dogtooth violets, Dutchman's-breeches, toothwort, bluebells, wild geraniums, snow trillium, and goldenrod.

Animals: White-tailed deer, mink, muskrats, raccoons, foxes, squirrels, rabbits, beavers, opossums, striped skunks

Birds: More than three hundred types of birds are found in Illinois, including bobwhite quails, ringneck pheasants, Canada geese, sparrows, American crows, red-winged blackbirds, hummingbirds, bluejays, and chickadees. Every spring and fall Illinoisans witness the migration of about 1 million waterfowl over the route known as the Mississippi Flyway.

Fish: The more than 180 species of fish that can be found in Illinois' lakes, streams, and rivers include bullheads, carp, catfish, salmon, lake trout, perch, smelt, buffalo fish, largemouth and smallmouth bass, crappies, bluegills, red-ear sunfish, white bass, walleyes, saugers, and northern pike.

GOVERNMENT

The government of Illinois, like the federal government, is divided into three branches—legislative, executive, and judicial. The state's legislative branch, the General Assembly, is made up of a Senate with 59 members and a House of Representatives with 118 members. The General Assembly creates new laws, rescinds or revises old ones, and works with the governor to prepare the state budget. It also has the power to impeach and remove judicial and executive officials. The state Senate can refuse to confirm appointments made by the governor. Voters elect state senators to terms of either two or four years. The terms are staggered so that the Senate cannot be completely changed in a single election. State representatives are elected to two-year terms.

The executive branch, headed by the governor, administers the law. The governor is elected to a four-year term. There is no limit to the number of terms a governor may serve. The state constitution gives the governor the authority to veto or approve laws passed by the General Assembly, to grant pardons, to serve as commander-in-chief of the state militia, and to call emergency sessions of the General Assembly. The governor also has the power to appoint hundreds of state administrators.

The judicial branch interprets laws and tries cases. The state has only three kinds of courts—supreme, appellate, and circuit. Illinois abolished all lower courts in 1964 and expanded the circuit courts to hear lower cases. Judges are elected by the voters. The supreme court is the highest tribunal in the state, and has seven justices elected to ten-year terms. Every three years, the supreme court justices elect one of their members to be chief justice. The thirty-six justices of the appellate court, which hears appeals from the circuit courts, are also elected to ten-year terms. There are twenty-one circuit courts in Illinois, presided over by varying numbers of circuit and associate judges. The circuit judges, who are elected to six-year terms, appoint the associate judges to four-year terms. One of Illinois' circuit courts, the Circuit Court of Cook County, has about 140 judges, making it the largest court in the United States.

Number of Counties: 102

U.S. Representatives: 22

Electoral Votes: 24

Voting Qualifications: Eighteen years of age, one year residency in state

EDUCATION

In 1985, one fourth of the Illinois state budget was spent on education. The state's public school system, established in 1825, is managed by a board of education with seventeen governor-appointed members. The board appoints a state superintendent. There are about 1,000 school districts and about 4,070 public schools in Illinois. Each district is controlled by a local board. Children between the ages of seven and sixteen are required to attend school. In 1983, there were 1.3 million grade-school students and more than half a million secondary-school students attending public schools in Illinois, at a cost of $2,904 per student.

About 15 percent of the students in Illinois attend nonpublic schools. The largest private-school system in the state is run by the Roman Catholic church. There are a number of well-known private schools in the Chicago area, including North Shore Country Day School, Francis W. Parker School, Latin School of Chicago, and University of Chicago Laboratory School.

Illinois has about 160 institutions of higher learning. There are 74 major universities and colleges, counting both public and private institutions. The largest university is the state-supported University of Illinois, which serves thirty-five thousand students at its main campus in Champaign-Urbana, and twenty thousand students at its Chicago campus. Other state-run universities are Northern Illinois at DeKalb, Southern Illinois at Carbondale and Edwardsville, Western Illinois at Macomb, Eastern Illinois at Charleston, Northeastern Illinois at Chicago, and Illinois State at Normal. Illinois also has a number of leading private schools, such as the prestigious University of Chicago, Northwestern University, Lake Forest College, and three Catholic schools—Loyola University, DePaul University, and Mundelein College. Other leading educational institutions are National College of Education, Illinois Institute of Technology, Columbia College, and the School of the Art Institute of Chicago.

ECONOMY AND INDUSTRY

Principal Products:

Agriculture: Corn, soybeans, hogs, beef cattle, sheep, milk, oats, wheat, alfalfa, barley, hay, rye, peaches, apples, and melons

Manufacturing: Non-electric machinery, farm equipment, electrical equipment and supplies, iron and steel, processed foods, fabricated metal products, paper products, printed materials, chemicals, medicines, athletic goods, candy, diesel engines, railroad equipment

Natural Resources: Fertile soil, forests, bituminous coal, fluorspar, peat, petroleum, clay, gravel, limestone, silica sand, tripoli, lead, zinc, natural gas, oil

Business and Trade: Chicago, the largest city in Illinois, is one of the country's leading trading centers with about 11,000 wholesale and 28,500 retail companies. The Merchandise Mart, a major wholesale buying center in Chicago, is the world's second-largest commercial building. The Chicago Board of Trade, which handles the contracts for 90 percent of the nation's future grain deliveries, is not only the largest grain exchange in the country, but is also the largest commodity exchange in the world. The Chicago Mercantile Exchange is the world's busiest market for future deliveries of perishable farm products such as eggs, cattle, and hogs.

Chicago is one of the nation's major convention and trade-show centers. About one thousand trade shows attracting half a million buyers are held each year. The city also handles 90 percent of the country's mail-order business.

Finance: Chicago is considered the financial capital of the Midwest. The city has one hundred state and federal banks, more than two hundred savings and loan companies, and four of the fifty largest commercial banking firms in the country. It is also the location of the Seventh Federal Reserve District Bank. Chicago's Midwest Stock Exchange is the third-largest securities market in the United States. Illinois is also a major insurance center, and is headquarters for two of the largest auto insurance companies in the world.

Communication: Illinois has about 100 daily and over 600 weekly newspapers, and about 770 periodicals. The two major daily newspapers in Chicago are the *Chicago Sun-Times* and the *Chicago Tribune.* Other important dailies are the *Alton Telegraph,* the *Bloomington Pantagraph,* the *State Journal-Register* of Springfield, the *Peoria Journal-Star,* the *Joliet Herald-News,* the *Chicago Daily Defender,* and Rockford's *Register Star.* The state has about 300 radio stations and 30 television stations. Its 1,700 printing firms make it an important center for book and magazine publishing and printing, especially in the areas of education, encyclopedias, medicine, and business.

Transportation: Illinois' central location has made it the transportation center of the United States. There are 95 public and 800 private airports in the state. Chicago's O'Hare International Airport, which encompasses 10 sq. mi. (26 km^2), is the busiest commercial airport in the world. About 2,000 planes and 131,000 passengers pass through the airport every day.

Illinois is also the center of the world's largest and busiest railroad network. There are about fifty industrial lines operating on 11,000 mi. (17,699 km) of track, and about thirteen passenger lines serving fifty cities and towns. In all, the state has 23,000 mi. (37,015 km) of track, the second highest in the nation. Commuter lines in the Chicago area carry about 250,000 passengers every weekday.

There are 133,000 mi. (214,000 km) of highways, roads, and streets, and the state is crossed by ten interstate routes and twenty-two U.S. highways.

Chicago has become one of the world's busiest inland ports since the 1959 opening of the St. Lawrence Seaway, which connects the Great Lakes to the Atlantic Ocean. Ships carry goods between Chicago and other Great Lakes ports, Central America, and Europe. Approximately 20 percent of the goods exported from the United States are sent from Chicago. Each year the Chicago Port Authority receives cargo ships and barges carrying 43 million short tons (39 metric tonnes) of manufactured goods, raw materials, and produce. The state's 1,200 mi. (1,931 km) inland waterway system is the most extensive in the country. Lake Michigan is linked to the Mississippi River by the Illinois Waterway, which includes the Chicago River, the Chicago Sanitary and Ship Canal, and the Des Plaines and Illinois rivers.

Concertgoers arrive at the gates of Ravinia, an outdoor pavilion and park in which pop, rock, jazz, blues, and symphony concerts are held during the summer.

SOCIAL AND CULTURAL LIFE

Museums: Along Chicago's lakefront there is a concentration of fine museums, including the Museum of Science and Industry, which features a realistic model of a coal mine and an authentic German submarine; the Adler Planetarium, the first planetarium in the Western Hemisphere; the Field Museum of Natural History; and the John G. Shedd Aquarium. The Art Institute of Chicago is best known for its magnificent collection of French impressionist paintings. Other art museums are the Museum of Contemporary Art in Chicago and the Terra Museum of American Art in Evanston. Historical museums include the Chicago Historical Society Museum, the Du Sable Museum of African American History in Chicago, the Illinois State Museum in Springfield, the Hauberg Indian Museum in Rock Island, and the Galena Historical Museum. Other important museums are the Lakeview Museum for Arts and Sciences in Peoria, the Oriental Institute Museum in Chicago, the Chicago Academy of Sciences, and the Burpee Museum of Natural History in Rockford, which contains artifacts of the Woodland Indian culture.

Libraries: There are 580 public libraries in the state. The central library of the public system is the Illinois State Library in Springfield, which supplements the holdings of other libraries, houses state archives, and provides a bookmobile program for rural areas. With 4.75 million volumes, the Chicago Public Library is not only the largest in the state, but the second-largest public library in the nation. The Illinois State Historical Library in Springfield houses special materials on Abraham Lincoln and the history of Illinois. Other major libraries are the University of Illinois Library at Champaign-Urbana, which houses 3.5 million volumes, and the University of Chicago Library, with 2.5 million volumes. Chicago has a number of private libraries, including the Newberry Library, which specializes in historical materials and rare books, and the John Crerar Library at the Illinois Institute of Technology, which has collections in the natural, physical, and social sciences.

Performing Arts: The Chicago Symphony Orchestra under the direction of Sir Georg Solti is considered by many to be the best symphony orchestra in the world. Chicago also has a major opera company, the Lyric Opera. Every summer, Chicago Symphony concerts are held at Ravinia, an outdoor pavilion in Highland Park. Pop, rock, jazz, and blues concerts are also featured at the Ravinia Festival. Free summer concerts are given by the Grant Park Symphony Orchestra at Grant Park on Chicago's lakefront.

Illinois has a number of excellent Chicago-based dance companies, including the Chicago City Ballet, the Hubbard Street Dance Company, the Chicago Repertory Dance Ensemble, and the Joseph Holmes Dance Theater. Training is offered at the Ruth Page Foundation School of Dance, MoMing Dance and Arts Center, the Chicago School of Ballet, Gus Giordano's Dance Center in Evanston, and many other schools.

Plays and musicals imported from Broadway and elsewhere are presented at a number of downtown Chicago theaters, including the Shubert, the Blackstone, the Auditorium, and the Arie Crown. It is the recent appearance of a number of "off-Loop" theaters and repertory companies, however, that has made Chicago one of the most exciting centers for theater in America. The Goodman Theater, Steppenwolf, and Wisdom Bridge are three Chicago companies that have achieved national recognition. Other important theaters are North Light, Body Politic, Remains, and the Organic Theatre Company. Chicago also has a long tradition of improvisational theater. Second City Theatre, which has been presenting improvisation-based revues for twenty-five years, was the first group of its kind, and has launched the careers of many famous actors and actresses.

Sports and Recreation: For professional sports entertainment, most Illinois residents follow the exploits of Chicago teams. The city has at least one team for every major sport: The National Football League (NFL) Bears; the National Basketball Association (NBA) Bulls; the National Hockey League (NHL) Blackhawks; and the Major Indoor Soccer League (MISL) Sting. An intense rivalry exists between Chicago's two professional baseball teams, the National League Cubs and the American League White Sox.

Illinois has two major zoos—Brookfield Zoo and Chicago's Lincoln Park Zoo. Each features animals in settings that attempt to imitate their natural habitats. The Botanic Garden of Chicago in Glencoe and the Morton Arboretum in Lisle contain a fascinating array of plants, trees, and wildlife. Great America, an amusement park in Gurnee, has some of the largest and fastest rides in the country.

Lake Michigan and the thousands of streams, rivers, and smaller lakes in the state provide excellent fishing, boating, and swimming. Hunting, camping, hiking, and other kinds of outdoor recreation are made possible by Illinois' extensive system of state parks and conservation areas. The state has seventy-two state parks, ninety-nine nature preserves, and thirty-nine conservation areas. Some of the more interesting state parks are Starved Rock State Park near Utica, known for its stunning, dramatic rock formations; Mississippi Palisades Park near Savanna, which features magnificent bluffs overlooking the Mississippi River; Illinois Beach State Park in Zion, a 3-mi. (4.8-km) stretch of sand dunes on Lake Michigan; and Lowden State Park in Oregon, the site of a famous statue of Black Hawk by Lorado Taft. Other popular state parks are Chain-O'Lakes, Apple River Canyon, Lincoln Trail, Argyle Lake, Black Hawk, and Fort Kaskaskia. The state has four state forests: Big River in western Illinois, Hidden Springs and Sand Ridge in central Illinois, and Trail of Tears in southern Illinois. One of the most beautiful areas in all of Illinois is Shawnee National Forest, which covers 260,000 acres (105,222 hectares) of forested hills and secluded valleys in the southernmost part of the state.

The Old Colony Church at Bishop Hill displays paintings by Bishop Hill artist Olof Krans.

Historic Sites And Landmarks:

Bishop Hill, near Galva, was the site of a religious commune founded in 1846 by a small group of Swedish immigrants led by a zealot named Erik Jansson. Dissension dissolved the community in 1861, but many of the old buildings have been restored, including the Steeple Building, which houses a museum; the Colony Church, which displays about a hundred paintings by the nineteenth-century Bishop Hill artist Olof Krans; and the Bjorklund Hotel.

Cahokia Mounds, near Collinsville, is the site of a city that was inhabited from A.D. 850 to 1500 by prehistoric Indians called the Mississippians by scientists. About sixty-five earthen ceremonial and burial mounds are preserved in the 1,800-acre (728-hectare) area, including Monk's Mound, the ceremonial center of the ancient community and the largest earthwork in the world.

John Deere Historic Site in Grand Detour includes the home and reconstructed blacksmith shop of John Deere, inventor of the first steel plow that was able to cut cleanly through prairie sod.

Fort de Chartres, near Prairie du Rocher, a massive French outpost built in 1720, was the center of civil and military government in the Illinois territory for more than fifty years. It was used in the French and Indian War and was ceded to the British in 1763. The original powder magazine there is the oldest building in Illinois.

Ulysses S. Grant Home in Galena is the house that the citizens of the town presented to Grant when he returned as a Civil War hero in 1865. The house contains some of the original furniture, and is decorated to look as it did when Grant lived there.

Hull House, on the Chicago campus of the University of Illinois, is the site of the original Hull House settlement founded by Jane Addams in 1889.

Abraham Lincoln studied law at night in the New Salem Village cooper shop.

Lincoln Log Cabin in Lerna was the last home of Abraham Lincoln's father and stepmother, Thomas and Sarah Lincoln.

Lincoln's Home in Springfield was the only house that Lincoln ever owned. He and his family lived there from 1844 until he became president in 1861.

Lincoln's Tomb at Oakridge Cemetery in Springfield is a beautiful memorial that is also the burial site of Lincoln's wife, Mary Todd Lincoln, and three of their sons.

Lovejoy Monument in Alton is a memorial commemorating the heroic actions of murdered abolitionist Elijah Lovejoy.

Nauvoo is a restoration of the remains of the Mormon community on the Mississippi River founded by Joseph Smith and lasting from 1839 to 1845. Points of interest are the ruins of the Mormon Temple on the hill; the graves of Joseph Smith and his family; and fifteen restored nineteenth-century buildings, including the homes of Joseph Smith and Brigham Young.

New Salem Village in Petersburg is a reproduction of the frontier village where Lincoln lived from 1831 to 1837. The original cooper shop where Lincoln studied law at night is there, as well as reconstructions of the Offut grocery store, where he worked as a clerk; the Lincoln-Berry store, of which he was part owner; and the post office where he served as postmaster.

Robie House in Chicago, built in 1909, is one of the best examples of Frank Lloyd Wright's prairie style of architecture.

The Vandalia Statehouse served as Illinois' state capitol building from 1836 to 1839.

Baha'i Temple in Wilmette, the North American headquarters of the Baha'i religion

Other Interesting Places to Visit:

Baha'i Temple in Wilmette is a beautiful domed structure that is the North American headquarters of the Baha'i religion.

Dickson Mounds, near Lewistown, are situated in a 63-acre (25-hectare) park. An unusual museum has been constructed over an excavated part of one mound, exposing the skeletons, tools, weapons, and artifacts of the ancient Indians in the exact positions in which they were buried.

The Governor's Mansion in Springfield is a two-and-a-half story brick residence that was built in the 1850s. The mansion has been restored by the state and furnished with antiques.

Lincoln Depot in Springfield is the spot where Lincoln made a moving speech to his friends before departing for his presidential inauguration in Washington, D.C.

The Old State Capitol in Springfield, built in 1837, was Illinois' third capitol. It was restored in 1968 to its original appearance. It was here that Lincoln made the speech that included the famous phrase "a house divided against itself cannot stand."

Carl Sandburg Birthplace in Galesburg is a three-room cottage that was bought in 1873 for $365 by Carl Sandburg's father, a Swedish immigrant. It reflects the writer's humble background. A room has been added in the back to display Sandburg exhibits and memorabilia.

The State Capitol in Springfield is the current seat of government in Illinois. This great domed building, completed in 1887, is designed in the shape of a Latin cross, and contains the house and senate chambers, as well as the governor's office.

IMPORTANT DATES

300 B.C.-A.D. 500—The mound-building Hopewell Culture flourishes

800-1500—The Mississippi Culture, another mound-building culture, becomes dominant

Late 1500s—The Illiniwek establish villages along the Illinois River and become the leading ethnic group in the region

1673—Marquette and Jolliet become the first Europeans to cross into present Illinois

Late 1600s—Pressure from the Iroquois causes the Sauk, Fox, Winnebago, and other tribes to move into Illiniwek territory

1680—Iroquois attack and kill many Illiniwek; French adventurer LaSalle establishes forts along the Illinois River

Early 1700s—French begin to settle along the Mississippi River in southern Illinois; they shorten the term Illiniwek Territory to Illinois

1717—Illinois region becomes part of the French colony of Louisiana

1763—Following defeat in the French and Indian War, France cedes much of its North American territory, including the Illinois region, to Great Britain

1770s—Jean Baptiste Point du Sable establishes a trading post at the shore of Lake Michigan near the Chicago River

1778—George Rogers Clark captures the British-held forts of Kaskaskia and Cahokia; the Illinois region becomes a county of Virginia

1783—The Illinois region is given to the newly formed United States of America as part of the treaty ending the American revolutionary war

1784—Virginia cedes the Illinois region to the United States government

1787—Congress passes the Northwest Ordinance, a brilliant act of legislation that encourages development of the Northwest Territory, of which Illinois becomes a part

1794—After losing the Battle of Fallen Timbers in Ohio, Indians are forced to sign the Treaty of Greenville giving the government control over key areas of the Midwest, including the sections of land that are today Chicago and Peoria

1800—The Indiana Territory, which includes the Illinois region, is created by congressional legislation

1803—United States troops build and occupy Fort Dearborn near du Sable's old settlement

1809—The Illinois Territory is created by an act of Congress; Kaskaskia becomes the first capital of the territory

1812—Fort Dearborn Massacre

1818—Illinois achieves statehood; first state constitution adopted; Kaskaskia chosen as first state capital; Shadrach Bond elected first governor

1820—State capital moves to Vandalia

1825—Erie Canal opens in New York, making it easier for settlers from the northeast to migrate to Illinois

1832—In the Black Hawk War, the Indians suffer a crushing defeat; the Sauk and Fox are driven from Illinois

1837—Springfield replaces Vandalia as the state capital; Chicago incorporated as a city; abolitionist Elijah Lovejoy murdered by mob in Alton; John Deere invents steel plow

1844—Joseph Smith murdered by anti-Mormon mob at Nauvoo

1848—Illinois-Michigan Canal connecting Lake Michigan to the Mississippi River system completed; second state constitution adopted

1853—General Assembly enacts oppressive "black laws" limiting the rights of blacks

1856—Illinois Central Railroad, then the longest railroad in the world, completed

1858—Lincoln-Douglas debates held in various cities throughout Illinois

1860—Lincoln elected president

1865—Illinois becomes the first state to ratify the Thirteenth Amendment, abolishing slavery; "black laws" repealed

1867—University of Illinois founded

1870—Third state constitution adopted

1871—The Great Chicago Fire razes the city, kills three hundred people, and leaves one hundred thousand homeless

1886—Haymarket Riot results from union-management conflict

In 1915, the excursion steamer *Eastland* capsized in the Chicago River, killing 812 passengers.

1889—Jane Addam's Hull House founded in Chicago

1893—Chicago hosts the World's Columbian Exposition

1894—Pullman Palace Car Company strike develops into a general railway strike; violence results and federal troops are called in

1900—Chicago Sanitary and Ship Canal opens, permanently reversing the flow of the Chicago River

1903—A fire in Chicago's Iroquois Theater kills 571 people; Illinois becomes the first state to establish the eight-hour workday and forty-hour workweek for children

1913—Illinois becomes the first state east of the Mississippi to grant women the right to vote in presidential elections

1915—The *Eastland,* an excursion steamer, capsizes in the Chicago River, killing 812 passengers

1917—Race riots in East St. Louis occur when the labor market is flooded with black laborers from the south; fifty people are killed

1919—The biggest race riot in Chicago history erupts when a young black boy drowns after not being permitted to swim ashore onto a "white" beach; twenty-four blacks and fifteen whites are killed and hundreds are injured

1929—St. Valentine's Day Massacre

1933—Chicago hosts the Century of Progress Exposition; Illinois Waterway opens

1942—Scientists at the University of Chicago launch the Atomic Age by setting in motion the first self-sustaining atomic chain reaction

1950—Chicago poet Gwendolyn Brooks becomes the first black woman to receive the Pulitzer Prize in poetry

1968—War protesters clash with police in the streets of Chicago during the Democratic National Convention

1970—Fourth state constitution adopted

1973—Sears Tower, the world's tallest building, completed

1979—Chicago elects its first woman mayor; in the nation's worst air disaster up to that time, 251 people are killed as a jet leaving O'Hare Field crashes upon take-off

1983—Chicago's first black mayor is elected

1987—Governor James R. Thompson inaugurated for an unprecedented fourth term

JANE ADDAMS

IMPORTANT PEOPLE

Jane Addams (1860-1935), born in Cedarville; social worker, social reformer, lecturer; fought for civil liberties and better living conditions; founded Hull House, a settlement facility in a poor, immigrant Chicago neighborhood; shared 1931 Nobel Peace Prize; helped found American Civil Liberties Union

Ivan Albright (1897-1983), born in Chicago; painter of dark and gloomy themes; masterpiece was *That Which I Should Have Done I Did Not Do*

Nelson Algren (1909-1981), fiction writer known for realistic portrayals of life in the Chicago slums; most acclaimed novel was *The Man with the Golden Arm*

JOHN ALTGELD

John Peter Altgeld (1847-1902), lawyer and liberal political leader; governor of Illinois (1893-97); worked for reform of working conditions, prison conditions, education; criticized for pardoning anarchists convicted of conspiracy in the Haymarket Riot

Sherwood Anderson (1876-1941), fiction writer; contributed to literary "Chicago Renaissance" of the early 1900s; best known for *Winesburg, Ohio, a* collection of short stories depicting life in small-town America

Philip Danforth Armour (1832-1901), Chicago industrialist; leading innovator in meat-packing industry; formed Armour & Company, one of world's largest meat-packing firms; founded Armour Institute of Technology

SAUL BELLOW

Saul Bellow (1915-   ), fiction and nonfiction writer; known for portrayal of Jewish life in contemporary America; received 1976 Nobel Prize in literature

BLACK HAWK

GWENDOLYN BROOKS

RICHARD J. DALEY

CLARENCE DARROW

Jack Benny (1894-1974), born Benjamin Kubelsky in Chicago; radio and television comedian who portrayed himself as a vain miser

Black Hawk (1767-1838), Sauk Indian born near what is now Rockford; last Indian leader to resist white settlement in Illinois; ally of British in War of 1812; defeated by United States militia in Black Hawk War

Shadrach Bond (1773-1832), first governor of Illinois

Gwendolyn Brooks (1917-   ), poet; grew up in Chicago; poet laureate of Illinois; voiced the frustrations of black people in America in such poetry collections as *A Street in Bronzeville;* received 1950 Pulitzer Prize in poetry for *Annie Allen*

William Jennings Bryan (1860-1925), born in Salem; lawyer, politician, orator, religious fundamentalist; made three unsuccessful bids for presidency of the United States; secretary of state under Woodrow Wilson; engaged in courtroom debate with Clarence Darrow while assisting the prosecution in the famous Scopes trial

Daniel Hudson Burnham (1846-1912), architect and city planner; chief architect of World's Columbian Exposition in Chicago; planned the use of Chicago's lakefront for recreational purposes; designed such notable Chicago buildings as the Montauk, Rookery, and Railway Exchange

Jane Margaret Byrne (1933-   ), born in Chicago; first woman mayor of Chicago (1979-83)

Saint Frances Xavier Cabrini (1850-1917), Roman Catholic nun; first American citizen to be canonized; founded Chicago's Columbus Hospital

Anton Joseph Cermak (1873-1933), mayor of Chicago (1931-33); killed by bullet intended for President-elect Franklin D. Roosevelt

Richard Joseph Daley (1902-1976), born in Chicago; mayor of Chicago for twenty-one years (1955 until his death); one of the most powerful political leaders in America; headed the Cook County Democratic Organization, the strongest political machine in the country; provided reliable city services and sparked economic revival through construction of downtown buildings and urban-renewal programs; withstood corruption scandals involving the police force and court system

Clarence Seward Darrow (1857-1938), brilliant defense attorney; in 1887 established Chicago law practice; first rose to prominence when defending Socialist leader Eugene Debs in a conspiracy trial; saved from execution Nathan Leopold and Richard Loeb, two young Chicagoans who killed a young boy to prove they could commit the perfect crime; in famous Scopes trial, defended schoolteacher John Scopes's right to teach the theory of evolution

Miles Dewey Davis, Jr. (1926-   ), born in Alton; jazz trumpet player

Charles Gates Dawes (1865-1951), vice-president of United States (1925-29), financier, diplomat; shared 1925 Nobel Peace Prize for solving problem of collecting German reparations after World War I; chairman of the board of City National Bank and Trust Company of Chicago from 1932 until his death

John Deere (1804-1886), farm equipment inventor and manufacturer; introduced first steel plow to cut cleanly through heavy prairie sod and first riding plow

Everett McKinley Dirksen (1896-1969), born in Pekin; influential United States senator known for his skill as an orator; Senate Republican leader from 1959 until his death

Walter Elias (Walt) Disney (1901-1966), born in Chicago; motion picture animator and producer; creator of Disneyland amusement park in California and Disney World in Florida

John Roderigo Dos Passos (1896-1970), born in Chicago; novelist; most famous work was *U.S.A.*, a trilogy spanning three decades of American life

Stephen Arnold Douglas (1813-1861), popular and skillful political leader; major force in American politics before Civil War; represented Illinois as United States congressman (1843-47) and as United States senator (1847-61); especially known for series of debates against Lincoln on issue of slavery during 1858 senatorial campaign; believed people of newly annexed territories should decide for themselves whether to allow slavery

Jean Baptiste Point du Sable (1745-1818), pioneer and trader; first person to build a permanent house near the mouth of the Chicago River; regarded as the founder of Chicago

James Thomas Farrell (1904-1979), born in Chicago; novelist best known for his trilogy *Studs Lonigan*, a realistic portrayal of lower-middle-class Irish life in Chicago

Enrico Fermi (1901-1954), physicist; one of chief architects of nuclear age; received 1938 Nobel Prize in physics; at University of Chicago built first nuclear reactor and directed first sustained nuclear chain reaction

George Washington Gale Ferris (1859-1896), born in Galesburg; engineer; invented Ferris wheel for World's Columbian Exposition

Eugene Field (1850-1895), poet and journalist; did most of his writing in Chicago; wrote one of America's first newspaper columns, "Sharps and Flats," for *Chicago Morning News;* best known for childhood poems such as "Little Boy Blue" and "Wynken, Blynken, and Nod"

EVERETT DIRKSEN

STEPHEN A. DOUGLAS

JEAN DU SABLE

ENRICO FERMI

MARSHALL FIELD

ULYSSES S. GRANT

ERNEST HEMINGWAY

JOHN JOHNSON

Marshall Field (1834-1906), merchant; established Marshall Field & Company in Chicago, which became world's largest retail store; remembered for insistence on high-quality merchandise and fairness to customers; pioneer of modern retail merchandising; introduced clearly marked prices and exchange policy (slogan was "Give the Lady What She Wants"); donated $9 million for establishment of Field Museum of Natural History in Chicago and gave ten acres (four hectares) of land for University of Chicago

Ulysses Simpson Grant (1822-1885), eighteenth president of United States; Civil War general; resident of Galena off and on from 1860 to 1881; entered Civil War as colonel of an Illinois volunteer regiment; rose to rank of lieutenant general; in 1864 named supreme commander of Union forces; led Union army to victory in closing months of war; in recognition of accomplishments, given title General of the Army; president (1868-76)

Ben Hecht (1894-1964), playwright, novelist, screenwriter; experiences as Chicago newspaperman provided material for many works, including *The Front Page* (coauthored by Charles MacArthur)

Ernest Miller Hemingway (1899-1961), born in Oak Park; novelist and short-story writer; famous for portrayal of disillusioned "Lost Generation" of World War I; received 1954 Nobel Prize in literature; works include *The Sun Also Rises, A Farewell to Arms, For Whom the Bell Tolls, The Old Man and the Sea*

James Butler (Wild Bill) Hickok (1837-1876), born in Troy Grove; frontiersman, scout, United States marshal; known for his courage and shooting ability

William Le Baron Jenney (1832-1907), architect and engineer; founder of Chicago school of architecture; designed ten-story Home Insurance Building in Chicago, world's first metal-frame skyscraper

John Harold Johnson (1918-), founder and president of Johnson Publishing Company in Chicago, the leading black-owned business in the United States; publisher of magazines *Ebony, Ebony Jr., Jet, EM*

James Jones (1921-1977), born in Robinson; author; received 1951 National Book Award for *From Here to Eternity*

Florence Kelley (1859-1932), social worker and social reformer; investigation of working conditions in Illinois led to 1893 Sweatshop Act, which limited working hours for women and banned child labor in Illinois; became state's first chief factory inspector

John Kinzie (1763-1828), one of earliest Chicago settlers; established a trading post in 1804 near Fort Dearborn on site of present-day Chicago

Abraham Lincoln (1809-1865), sixteenth president of United States (1860-65); moved with parents to Illinois at age twenty-one; settled in New Salem; worked as a storekeeper, postmaster, surveyor while studying law; member of Illinois legislature (1834-41); moved to Springfield and opened law practice; "rode the circuit" trying legal cases throughout Illinois; served one term in United States House of Representatives (1846-49); in 1858, during an unsuccessful bid for United States Senate seat, engaged in famous debates with Stephen Douglas; in 1860 elected president of the United States; guided country through Civil War; in 1863 issued Emancipation Proclamation freeing slaves; assassinated by John Wilkes Booth five days after end of war

ABRAHAM LINCOLN

Vachel Lindsay (1879-1931), born in Springfield; poet; work characterized by strong rhythms and romantic themes; made long tours on foot through American countryside exchanging poetry readings for food and lodgings

Elijah Parish Lovejoy (1802-1837), newspaperman and abolitionist; publisher of *Alton Observer*, a newspaper attacking slavery; helped organize Illinois Anti-Slavery Society; was shot and killed while trying to stop angry mob from destroying his press

VACHEL LINDSAY

Archibald MacLeish (1892-1982), born in Glencoe; Pulitzer Prize-winning poet, dramatist, and critic

David Mamet (1947-), born in Chicago; playwright; received 1984 Pulitzer Prize in drama for *Glengarry Glen Ross*

Edgar Lee Masters (1869-1950), poet; contributed to literary Chicago Renaissance of early 1900s; drew on sights in and around his hometown of Lewistown, Illinois as an inspiration for his most famous work, *Spoon River Anthology*

William Henry (Bill) Mauldin (1921-), widely syndicated Pulitzer Prizewinning editorial cartoonist for the *Chicago Sun-Times*

EDGAR LEE MASTERS

Cyrus Hall McCormick (1809-1884), inventor and industrialist; invented and patented reaping machine with all essential elements of today's models; formed McCormick Harvesting Machine Company, eventually largest manufacturer of harvesting machines in the world

Robert Rutherford McCormick (1880-1955), born in Chicago; editor and publisher (with cousin Joseph Medill Patterson) of *Chicago Tribune* for forty-eight years; also founded *Washington Herald-Tribune* and (with Patterson) the *New York Daily News*

Joseph Medill (1823-1899), editor and publisher; in 1874 gained control of *Chicago Tribune;* made it one of most successful newspapers in the world; mayor of Chicago (1871-74); helped establish Chicago Public Library; major force in making Chicago site of World's Columbian Exposition

CYRUS McCORMICK

MIES VAN DER ROHE

HARRIET MONROE

POTTER PALMER

JULIUS ROSENWALD

Ludwig Mies van der Rohe (1886-1969), German-born architect; leader of International style of architecture; came to America in 1937; became head of architecture department of Illinois Institute of Technology (IIT) in Chicago; designed new campus for IIT; notable buildings in Chicago include the Federal Center and twin apartment buildings at 860 and 880 Lake Shore Drive

Harriet Monroe (1860-1936), born in Chicago; founder and editor of *Poetry: A Magazine of Verse;* published early works of such poets as T.S. Eliot, Ezra Pound, Wallace Stevens

Dwight Lyman Moody (1837-1899), evangelist and founder of nondenominational Moody Memorial Church, Moody Bible Institute, and Moody Press in Chicago; as president of Young Men's Christian Association (YMCA) built Farwell Hall in Chicago, first YMCA building in America

Benjamin Franklin (Frank) Norris (1870-1902), born in Chicago; muckraker novelist and journalist; exposed evils of urban-American society in such novels as *The Octopus, McTeague,* and *The Pit*

Potter Palmer (1826-1902), merchant and real-estate promoter; pioneer of modern selling methods; owned Chicago retail store that later became Marshall Field & Company; built Palmer House, a famous Chicago hotel; helped develop Chicago's State Street into major retail center

Allan Pinkerton (1819-1884), investigator; in Chicago opened first detective agency in United States; uncovered plot to assassinate President-elect Lincoln; guarded Lincoln on inaugural journey from Springfield to Washington, D.C.

George Mortimer Pullman (1831-1897), inventor and industrialist; improved and nationally marketed railway sleeping car; organized Pullman Palace Car Company; founded company town of Pullman, Illinois (now part of Chicago)

Ronald Wilson Reagan (1911-   ), born in Tampico; fortieth president of United States; grew up in Dixon; graduated from Eureka College; president of Screen Actors Guild (1947-52, 1959-60); governor of California (1967-75); president (1981-   )

Julius Rosenwald (1862-1932), born in Springfield; president (1909-24) and chairman of the board (1925 until death) of Sears, Roebuck & Company; contributed $63 million to a wide range of organizations; set aside $22.5 million for fund to improve opportunities for blacks in America; presented Chicago with Museum of Science and Industry

Mike Royko (1932-   ), born in Chicago; *Chicago Tribune* syndicated newspaper columnist; wrote for *Chicago Daily News* (1959-78) and *Chicago Sun-Times* (1978-84); received 1972 Pulitzer Prize in commentary

Carl Sandburg (1878-1967), born in Galesburg; poet and biographer; regarded as representative poet of Midwest and voice of American common man; traveled as hobo throughout the country collecting and singing American folk songs; worked as newspaper reporter in Milwaukee and Chicago; spent thirty years writing six-volume biography of Lincoln; received 1940 Pulitzer Prize in history for second part of biography (*Abraham Lincoln: The War Years*); wrote poems celebrating agricultural and industrial America; collections include *Good Morning, America; Smoke and Steel; The People, Yes;* received 1951 Pulitzer Prize in poetry for *Complete Poems*

CARL SANDBURG

Upton Beall Sinclair (1878-1968), muckraker novelist; most famous novel, *The Jungle,* exposed appalling conditions in Chicago meat-packing industry and led to passage of America's first pure-food laws

Joseph Smith (1805-1844), founder and first president of Mormon church; with followers founded Mormon community of Nauvoo; killed by angry mob after disagreement arose over his endorsement of polygamy

ADLAI E. STEVENSON

Adlai Ewing Stevenson (1900-1965), political leader known for eloquence, intelligence, and sharp wit; as young man worked on family newspaper, *Bloomington Daily Pantagraph;* practiced law in Chicago; delegate to United Nations (1946-47); governor of Illinois (1949-53); Democratic candidate for president of United States in 1952 and 1956, lost both times to Dwight D. Eisenhower; United States ambassador to United Nations (1961-65)

Louis Henri Sullivan (1856-1924), architect; leader of Chicago school of architecture; believed that function of a building should determine its form; famous buildings in Chicago include Auditorium Building (built with Dankmar Adler), Transportation Building at World's Columbian Exposition, and Carson Pirie Scott & Company Building

LOUIS SULLIVAN

Gustavus Franklin Swift (1836-1903), founder of Swift & Company, a world-famous Chicago meat-packing company

Louis (Studs) Terkel (1912-), social historian and Pulitzer Prizewinning author; worked for Federal Writer's Project during Great Depression; author of American oral histories such as *Hard Times, Working, The Good War;* host of "Studs Terkel Show," long-running Chicago radio interview program

Aaron Montgomery Ward (1843-1913), founded Chicago's Montgomery Ward & Company, world's first mail-order business; noted for successful efforts to preserve Chicago's Grant Park

Harold Washington (1922-1987), born in Chicago; member of United States House of Representatives (1981-83); first black mayor of Chicago (1983-1987)

STUDS TERKEL

DANIEL HALE WILLIAMS

FRANK LLOYD WRIGHT

Daniel Hale Williams (1856-1931), pioneering Chicago surgeon; helped improve opportunities for blacks in medicine; first surgeon to close successfully a tear in the sac around the human heart; founded Chicago's Provident Hospital, country's first interracial hospital and training center for black nurses and interns

Frank Lloyd Wright (1867-1959), architect; believed a building should reflect and fit into its environment; began in Chicago as assistant to Louis Sullivan; left to establish own practice; designed and built "prairie-style" structures in and around Chicago, such as Robie House in Chicago and Unity Temple in Oak Park; founded Taliesin Fellowship for training architecture students; continued to develop unique style in later buildings such as Kaufmann "Falling Water" house in Pennsylvania, Johnson Wax Company building in Wisconsin, and Guggenheim Museum in New York City

William Wrigley, Jr. (1861-1932), in Chicago founded William Wrigley Jr. Company, maker of chewing gum

Brigham Young (1801-1877), Mormon missionary; led fifteen thousand Mormons to Illinois after they were driven from Missouri; became leader of Mormon church after murder of Joseph Smith; led Mormons to Utah when forced to leave Illinois

GOVERNORS

Shadrach Bond	1818-1822
Edward Coles	1822-1826
Ninian Edwards	1826-1830
John Reynolds	1830-1834
William L.D. Ewing	1834
Joseph Duncan	1834-1838
Thomas Carlin	1838-1842
Thomas Ford	1842-1846
Augustus C. French	1846-1853
Joel Aldrich Matteson	1853-1857
William H. Bissell	1857-1860
John Wood	1860-1861
Richard Yates	1861-1865
Richard J. Oglesby	1865-1869
John M. Palmer	1869-1873
Richard J. Oglesby	1873
John L. Beveridge	1873-1877
Shelby Moore Cullom	1877-1883
John M. Hamilton	1883-1885
Richard J. Oglesby	1885-1889
Joseph W. Fifer	1889-1893
John P. Altgeld	1893-1897
John R. Tanner	1897-1901
Richard Yates	1901-1905
Charles S. Deneen	1905-1913
Edward F. Dunne	1913-1917
Frank O. Lowden	1917-1921
Len Small	1921-1929
Louis L. Emmerson	1929-1933
Henry Horner	1933-1940
John H. Stelle	1940-1941
Dwight H. Green	1941-1949
Adlai E. Stevenson	1949-1953
William G. Stratton	1953-1961
Otto Kerner	1961-1968
Samuel H. Shapiro	1968-1969
Richard B. Olgilvie	1969-1973
Daniel Walker	1973-1977
James R. Thompson	1977-

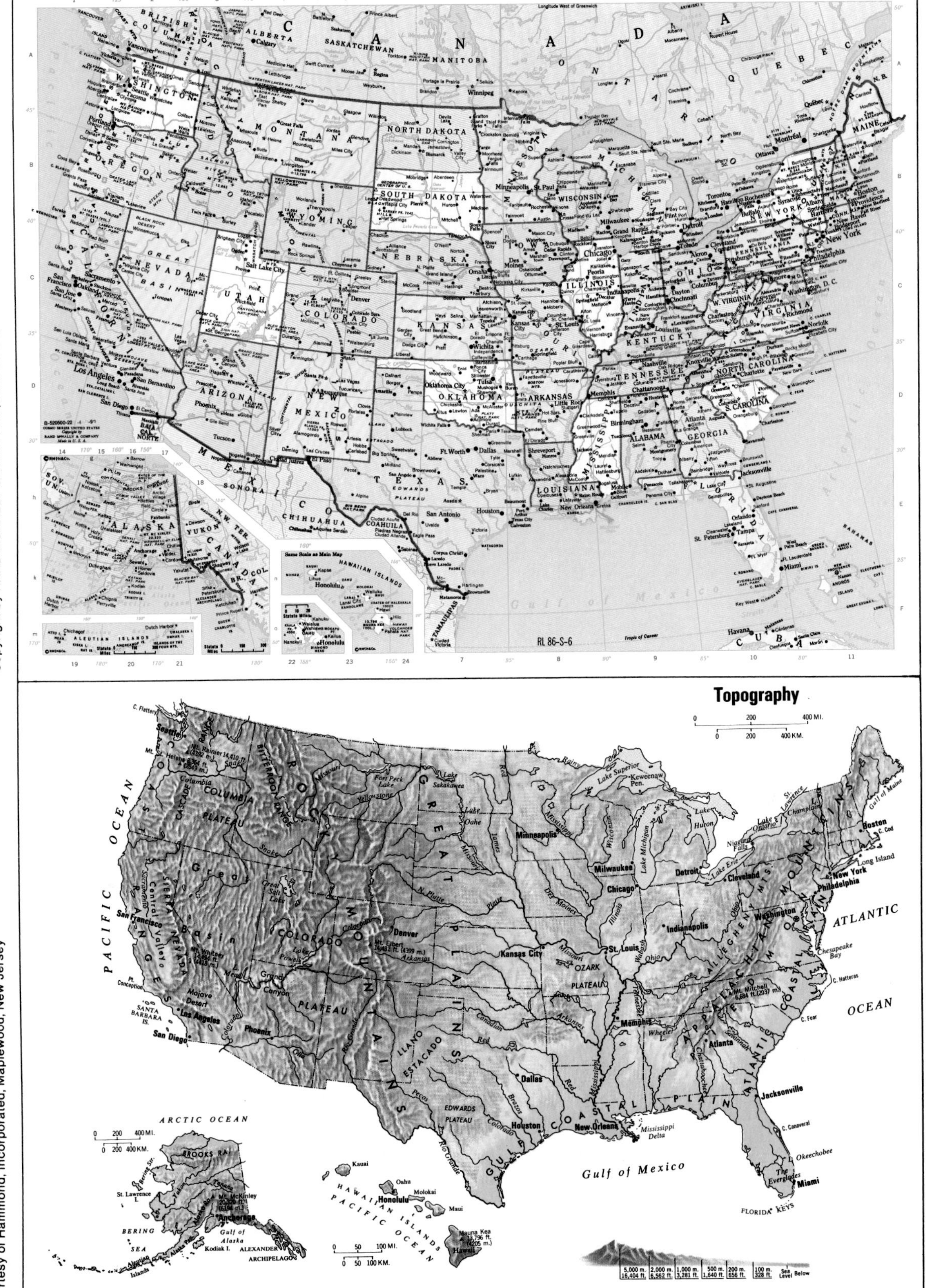
C A N A D A
RL 86-S-6
Gulf of Mexico
Topography
PACIFIC OCEAN
ATLANTIC OCEAN
ARCTIC OCEAN
BERING SEA
Gulf of Alaska
HAWAIIAN ISLANDS
PACIFIC OCEAN
ROCKY MOUNTAINS
GREAT PLAINS
COLUMBIA PLATEAU
COLORADO PLATEAU
OZARK PLATEAU
EDWARDS PLATEAU
LLANO ESTACADO
GULF COASTAL PLAIN
ATLANTIC COASTAL PLAIN
APPALACHIAN MOUNTAINS
PIEDMONT
Great Basin
FLORIDA KEYS
Mississippi Delta
Gulf of Maine
Chesapeake Bay
5,000 m. 16,404 ft.
2,000 m. 6,562 ft.
1,000 m. 3,281 ft.
500 m. 1,640 ft.
200 m. 656 ft.
100 m. 328 ft.
Sea Level
Below

MAP KEY

Abingdon	C3
Addison	k9
Aledo	B3
Algonquin	A5;h8
Allerton	D6
Alma	E5
Alton	E3
Anna	F4
Antioch	A5;h8
Arcola	D5
Arlington Heights	A5,6;h9
Arrowsmith	C5
Auburn	D4
Aurora	B5;k8
Barrington	A5;h8
Bartlett	k8
Bartonville	C4
Batavia	B5;k8
Beardstown	C3
Belleville	E4
Bellwood	k9
Belvidere	A5
Bensenville	B6;k9
Benton	E,F5
Berwyn	k9
Bethalto	E3
Big Muddy (river)	F4
Bloomingdale	k8
Bloomington	C4,5
Blue Island	B6;k9
Burbonnais	B6
Bradley	B6
Braidwood	B5
Breese	E4
Brookfield	k9
Bushnell	C3
Cahokia	E3
Cairo	F4
Calumet City	B6;k9
Calumet Sag Channel	k9
Canton	C3
Carbondale	F4
Carlinville	D4
Carlyle	E4
Carlyle Reservoir	E4
Carmi	E5
Carpentersville	A5;h8
Carrolton	D3
Carterville	F4
Carthage	C2
Cary	A5;h8
Casey	D6
Centralia	E4
Centreville	E3
Champaign	C5
Channahon	B5
Chanute Air Force Base	C5
Charles Mound	A3
Charleston	D5
Chatham	D4
Chester	F4
Chicago	B6;k9
Chicago Heights	B6;k9
Chicago Sanitary & Ship Canal	k,m8,9
Chillicothe	C4
Christopher	F4
Cicero	B6;k9
Clarendon Hills	k9
Clinton	C5
Coal City	B5
Coalton	D4
Collinsvile	E4
Columbia	E3
Crab Orchard Lake	F4
Crane Lake	C3
Crete	B6;m9
Creve Coeur	C4
Crystal Lake	A5;h8
Danville	C6
Decatur	D5
Deerfield	h9
De Kalb	B5
Des Plaines	A6;h9
Des Plaines (river)	h,k,m 8,9
Dixon	B4
Dolton	k9
Downers Grove	B5;k8
Dundee	A5;h8
Du Page (river)	k,m8
Dupo	E3
Du Quoin	E4
Dwight	B5
East Alton	E3
East Moline	B3
East Peoria	C4
East St. Louis	E3
Edwardsville	E4
Effingham	D5
Egypt Reservoir	F5
Eldorado	F5
Elgin	A5;h8
Elk Grove Village	h9
Elmhurst	B6;k9
Elmwood Park	k9
El Paso	C4
Embarrass (river)	D,E5,6
Eureka	C4
Evanston	A6;h9
Evergreen Park	k9
Fairbury	C5
Fairfield	E5
Farmington	C3
Flora	E5
Flossmoor	k9
Forest Park	k9
Fort Sheridan	h9
Fox (river)	A,B5,6;h,k8
Fox Lake	A5,h8
Fox River Grove	h8
Frankfort	m9
Franklin Park	k9
Freeburg	E4
Freeport	A4
Fulton	B3
Galena	A3
Galesburg	C3
Galva	B3
Geneseo	B3
Geneva	B5;k8
Genoa	A5
Georgetown	D6
Gibson City	C5
Gillespie	D4
Glen Ellyn	k8
Glencoe	A6;h9
Glenview	h9
Glenview Naval Air Station	h9
Granite City	E3
Grass Lake	h8
Grayslake	A6;h8
Great Lakes Training Center	h9
Green (river)	B3,4
Green Rock	B3
Greenville	E4
Gurnee	h9
Hamilton	C2
Harrisburg	F5
Harvard	A5
Harvey	B6;k9
Havana	C3
Hazel Crest	k9
Henry	B4
Herrin	F4
Hidalgo	D5
Highland	E4
Highland Park	A6;h9
Highwood	A6;h9
Hillsboro	D4
Hinsdale	k9
Hoffman Estates	h8
Homewood	B6;k9
Hoopeston	C6
Illinois (river)	B,C,D,E3,4,5,6
Illinois City	B3
Itasca	k8
Jacksonville	D3
Jerseyville	D3
Johnston City	F5
Joliet	B5;k8
Kankakee	B6
Kankakee (river)	B5, 6
Kaskaskia	F4
Kaskaskia (river)	D,E4,5
Kenilworth	h9
Kewanee	B4
Kickapoo Creek	C4,5
Kinderhook	D2
Kishwaukee (river)	A5
Knoxville	C3
La Grange	B6;k9
La Grange Park	k9
Lake Bloomington	C5
Lake Bluff	A6;h9
Lake Calumet	k9
Lake Decatur	D5
Lake Forest	A6;h9
Lake Kinkaid	D4
Lake Mattoon	D5
Lake Michigan	A,B6,7;h,k9,10
Lake Springfield	D4
Lake Villa	h8
Lake Zurich	h8
La Moine (river)	C3
Lansing	B6;k9
La Salle	B4
Lawrenceville	E6
Lebanon	E4
Lemont	B5;6;k9
Le Roy	C5
Lewistown	C3
Libertyville	A6;h9
Lincoln	C4
Lincolnshire	h9
Lincolnwood	h9
Lindenhurst	h8
Lisle	k8
Litchfield	D4
Little Muddy (river)	E4
Little Wabash (river)	E,F5
Lockport	B5;k8
Lombard	k8
Loves Park	A4
Lyons	k9
Mackinaw (river)	C4
Macomb	C3
Madison	E3
Manteno	B6
Marengo	A5
Marion	F5
Marissa	E4
Markham	k9
Marquette Heights	C4
Marseilles	B5
Marshall	D6
Mascoutah	E4
Mason City	C4
Matteson	k9
Mattoon	D5
Maywood	k9
McHenry	A5;h8
McLeansboro	E5
Melrose Park	F2
Mendota	B4
Metropolis	F5
Midlothian	k9
Midway Airport	k9
Milan	B3
Millstadt	E3
Mississippi (river)	A,B,C,D,E,F 2,3,4
Mokena	k9
Moline	B3
Momence	B6
Monmouth	C3
Montgomery	B5;k8
Monticello	C5
Morris	B5
Morrison	B4
Morton	C4
Morton Grove	h9
Mount Carmel	E6
Mount Morris	A4
Mount Prospect	A6;h9
Mount Vernon	E5
Mount Zion	D5
Mundelein	A6;h9
Murphysboro	F4
Naperville	B5;k8
Nashville	E4
New Lenox	B6;k9
Newton	E5
Niles	h9
Nokomis	D4
Normal	C4,5
Norridge	k9
North Aurora	k8
North Chicago	A6;h9
Northbrook	h9
North Fork (river)	E,F5
Northlake	k9
North Park	A4
Oak Forest	k9
Oak Lawn	B6;k9
Oak Park	B6;k9
O'Fallon	E4
Oglesby	B4
O'Hare International Airport	k9
Ohio (river)	F4,5
Olney	E5
Oregon	A4
Orland Park	k9
Oswego	B5;k8
Ottawa	B5
Palatine	A5;h8
Palos Park	k9
Pana	D4
Paris	D6
Park Forest	B6;m9
Park Ridge	A6;h9
Parkersburg	E5
Pawnee	D4
Paw Paw	B5
Paxton	C5
Pecatonica (river)	A4
Pekin	C4
Peoria	C4
Peoria Heights	C4
Peotone	B6
Peru	B4
Phoenix	k9
Pinkneyville	E4
Pittsfield	D3
Plainfield	B5;k8
Plainville	D2
Plano	B5
Polo	B4
Pontiac	C5
Posen	k9
Princeton	B4
Prophetstown	B4
Quincy	D2
Rantoul	C5
Red Bud	E4
Rend Lake	E4,5
Riverdale	k9
River Forest	k9
River Grove	k9
Riverside	k9
Riverton	D4
Riverwoods	h9
Robbins	k9
Robinson	D6
Rochelle	B4
Rock (river)	A,B3,4
Rock Creek	A,B3,4
Rock Falls	B4
Rockford	A4
Rock Island	B3
Rolling Meadows	h8
Rome	C4
Romeoville	B5;k8
Roselle	k8
Round Lake	h8
Round Lake Beach	h8
Rushville	C3
St. Charles	B5;k8
Salem	E5
Saline (river)	F4,5
Salt Creek	C4,5
Sandwich	B5
Sangamon (river)	C3,4
Savanna	A3
Scales Mound	A3
Schaumburg	h8
Schiller Park	k9
Scott Air Force Base	E4
Shawneetown	F5
Shelbyville	D5
Shelbyville Reservoir	D5
Shorewood	k8
Silvis	B3
Skillet Fork (river)	E5
Skokie	A6;h9
South Beloit	A4
South Chicago Heights	m9
South Elgin	B5;h,k8
South Holland	k9
South Jacksonville	D3
Sparta	E4
Spoon (river)	C3,4
Spring (lake)	C4
Springfield	D4
Spring Valley	B4
Staunton	D4
Steger	B6;m9
Sterling	B4
Stockland	C6
Streator	B5
Sullivan	D5
Summit	k9
Swansea	E4
Sycamore	B5
Taylorville	D4
Tinley Park	k9
Trenton	E4
Troy	E4
Tuscola	D5
Urbana	C5
Vandalia	E4
Venice	E3
Vernon Hills	h9
Villa Grove	D5
Villa Park	k9
Virden	D4
Wabash (river)	D,E,F5,6
Warrenville	k8
Washington	C4
Washington Park	E3
Waterloo	E3
Watseka	C6
Wauconda	h8
Waukegan	A6;h9
West Chicago	k8
Westchester	k9
Western Springs	k9
West Frankfort	F5
Westmont	k9
West Peoria	C4
Westville	C6
Wheaton	B5;k8
Wheeling	h9
White Hall	D3
Willow Springs	k9
Wilmette	A6;h9
Wilmington	B5
Winnetka	A6;h9
Wonder Lake	A5;h8
Wood Dale	k9
Wood River	E3
Woodstock	A5
Worth	k9
Yorkville	B5
Zion	A6;h9

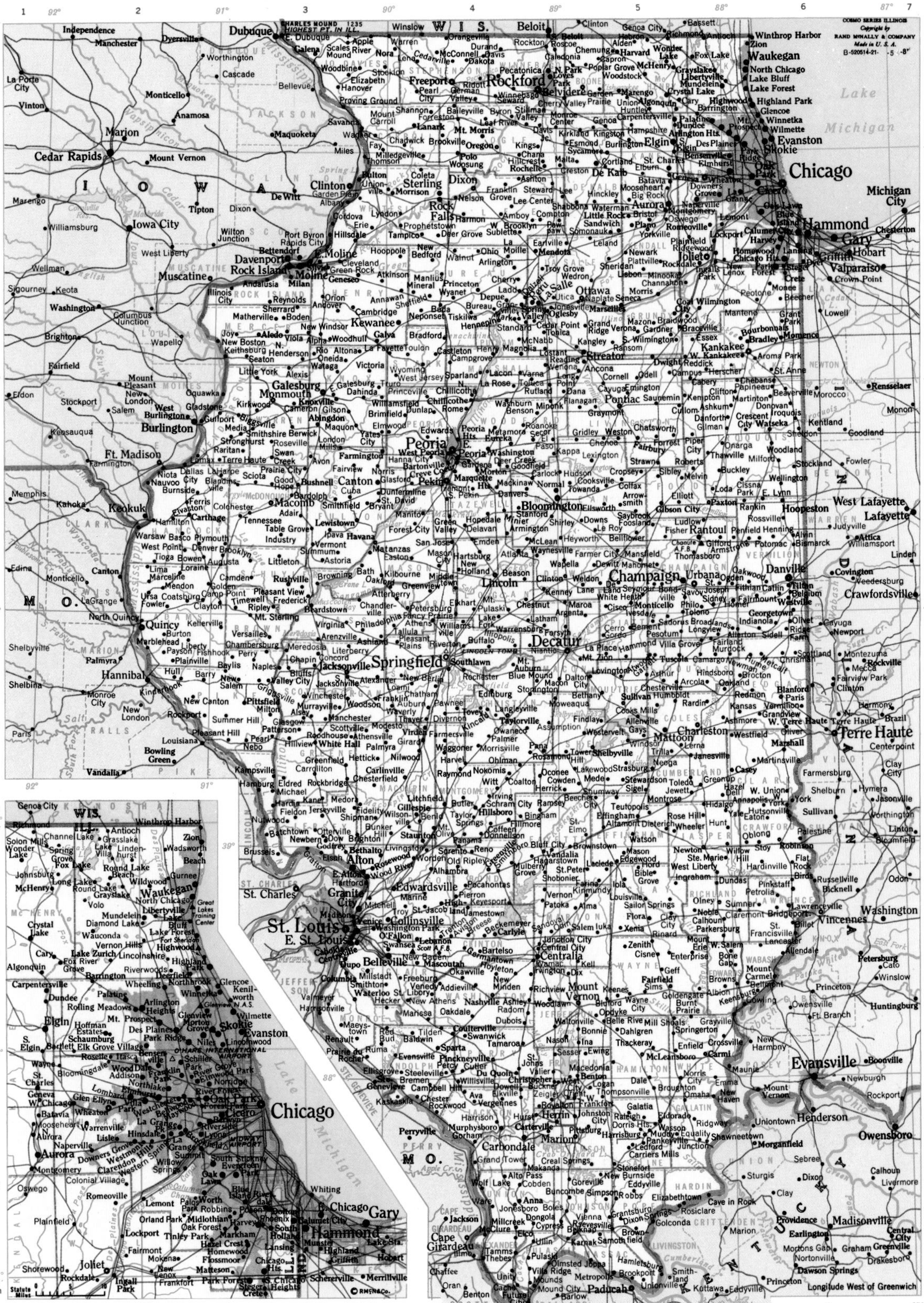

COSMO SERIES ILLINOIS
Copyright by
RAND McNALLY & COMPANY
Made in U. S. A.
B-520514-21- -5 -8"

CHARLES MOUND 1235 HIGHEST PT. IN ILL.

Statute Miles 5 0 5 10 20 30 40

Kilometers 5 0 5 15 25 35 45 55

Lambert Conformal Conic Projection

Longitude West of Greenwich

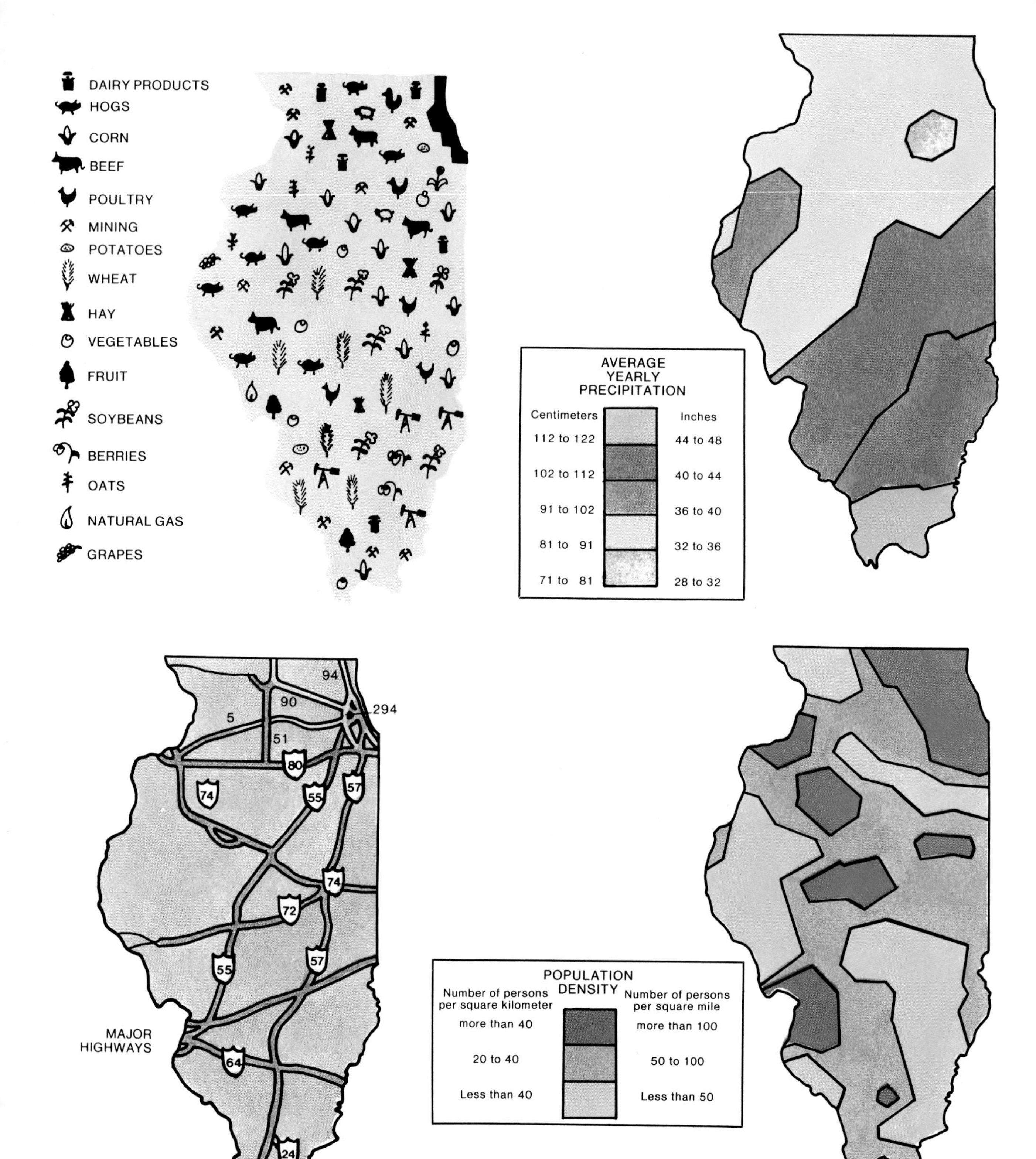
DAIRY PRODUCTS
HOGS
CORN
BEEF
POULTRY
MINING
POTATOES
WHEAT
HAY
VEGETABLES
FRUIT
SOYBEANS
BERRIES
OATS
NATURAL GAS
GRAPES
AVERAGE YEARLY PRECIPITATION
Centimeters
Inches
112 to 122
44 to 48
102 to 112
40 to 44
91 to 102
36 to 40
81 to 91
32 to 36
71 to 81
28 to 32
94
90
294
5
51
80
74
55
57
74
72
55
57
64
24
MAJOR HIGHWAYS
POPULATION DENSITY
Number of persons per square kilometer
Number of persons per square mile
more than 40
more than 100
20 to 40
50 to 100
Less than 40
Less than 50

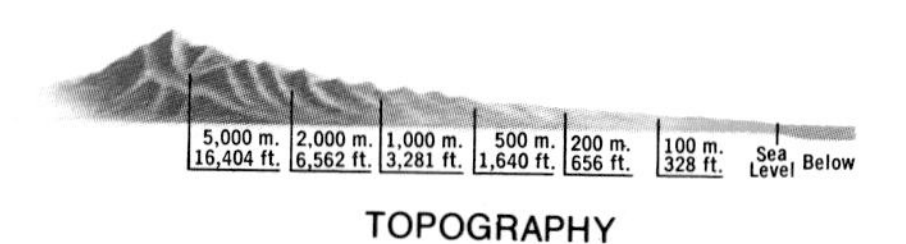

TOPOGRAPHY

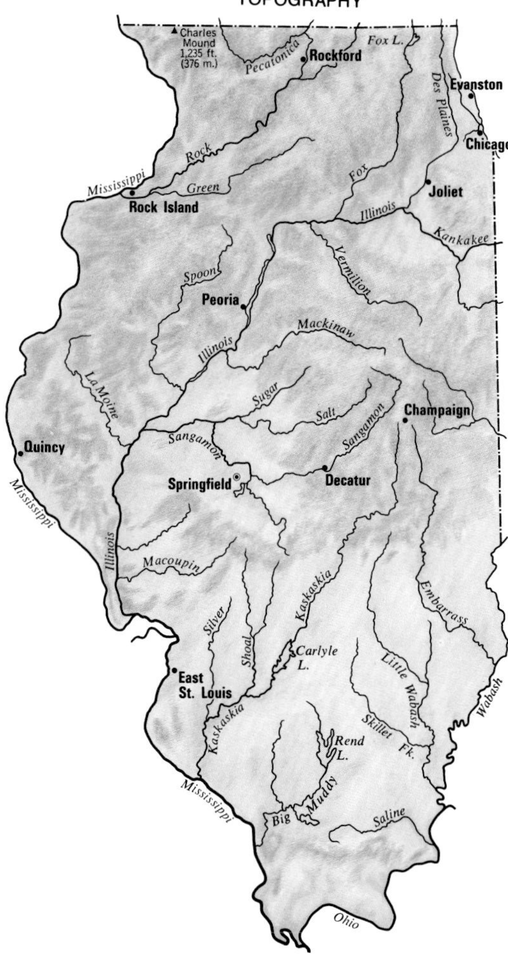

Courtesy of Hammond, Incorporated
Maplewood, New Jersey

COUNTIES

Galena JO DAVIESS; STEPHENSON Freeport; WINNEBAGO Rockford; BOONE Belvidere; MC HENRY Woodstock; LAKE
Mt Carroll CARROLL; OGLE Oregon; Sycamore DE KALB; KANE Geneva; Wheaton DU PAGE; COOK
Morrison WHITESIDE; Dixon LEE; Yorkville KENDALL; Joliet WILL
ROCK ISLAND; HENRY Cambridge; BUREAU Princeton; LA SALLE Ottawa; Morris GRUNDY
Aledo MERCER; Hennepin PUTNAM; KANKAKEE Kankakee
Toulon STARK; MARSHALL Lacon
HENDERSON; Monmouth WARREN; Galesburg KNOX; Pontiac LIVINGSTON; Watseka IROQUOIS
PEORIA Peoria; WOODFORD Eureka
Carthage HANCOCK; Macomb MC DONOUGH; FULTON Lewistown; Pekin TAZEWELL; MC LEAN Bloomington; FORD Paxton
Havana MASON; VERMILION Danville
SCHUYLER Rushville; Lincoln LOGAN; DE WITT Clinton; Urbana CHAMPAIGN
Mt Sterling ADAMS Quincy; BROWN; CASS Virginia; MENARD Petersburg; PIATT Monticello
SPRINGFIELD SANGAMON; MACON Decatur; Tuscola DOUGLAS
Jacksonville MORGAN; SCOTT Winchester; Pittsfield PIKE
MOULTRIE Sullivan; EDGAR Paris
Taylorville CHRISTIAN; SHELBY Shelbyville; COLES Charleston
GREENE Carrollton; Carlinville MACOUPIN; MONTGOMERY Hillsboro; Marshall CLARK; CUMBERLAND Toledo
CALHOUN Hardin; Jerseyville JERSEY
Effingham EFFINGHAM; FAYETTE Vandalia; JASPER Newton; Robinson CRAWFORD
BOND Greenville
MADISON Edwardsville; Louisville CLAY; Olney RICHLAND; LAWRENCE
CLINTON Carlyle; MARION Salem
Belleville ST CLAIR; WAYNE Fairfield; EDWARDS Albion; WABASH
Nashville WASHINGTON; Mt Vernon JEFFERSON
Waterloo MONROE
RANDOLPH Chester; PERRY Pinckneyville; McLeansboro HAMILTON; FRANKLIN Benton; Carmi WHITE
JACKSON Murphysboro; Marion WILLIAMSON; SALINE Harrisburg; GALLATIN
UNION Jonesboro; JOHNSON Vienna; POPE; HARDIN
ALEXANDER; PULASKI; MASSAC Metropolis

Winter on the Fox River

INDEX

Page numbers that appear in boldface type indicate illustrations

The dragon dance is the highlight of the annual summer fair in Chicago's Chinatown.

Picture Identifications

Front cover: Chicago Loop skyline with Lincoln Park in the foreground and the shore of Lake Michigan on the left
Back cover: The Fox River
Pages 2-3: Goose Lake Prairie Indian Grass at sunset.
Page 6: Galena
Pages 8-9: Farm and pond
Pages 18-19: Montage of the ethnic mosaic of Illinois
Page 26: The Koster Site excavation
Pages 38-39: Pioneers moving their possessions up a river on a flatboat
Page 53: A view from Lake Michigan showing Chicago at the height of the Great Chicago Fire
Page 68: The Illinois State Capitol Building, Springfield
Pages 78-79: North Chicago Loop area looking toward Lake Michigan
Page 88: The lions in front of the Art Institute decked out in Chicago Bears football team helmets to honor the 1985-86 Super Bowl champions
Page 96 (inset): Sears Tower
Pages 96-97: Young corn near Grayslake
Page 108: Montage showing the state flag, the state bird (cardinal), the state tree (white oak), the state flower (native violet), and the state animal (white-tailed deer)

About the Author

R. Conrad Stein, a native Illinoisan, was born in Chicago and educated at the University of Illinois at Champaign-Urbana. He has tried living in other parts of the world, but he continually returns to his home state. He now lives in Chicago with his wife and their daughter, Janna. Mr. Stein is the author of many other books, articles, and short stories written for young readers. To prepare for this book Mr. Stein toured the state, revisiting places he had not seen in years and discovering many sites he had never seen before. Even a lifetime resident such as Mr. Stein can find Illinois an exciting state to explore.

Picture Acknowledgments

© **Robert Frerck/Odyssey Productions**, Chicago: Front cover, pages 19 (bottom left and bottom right), 92 (right)
© **Jerry Hennen:** Back cover, pages 8-9, 16 (top left)
© **James P. Rowan:** Pages 2-3, 6, 14, 16 (top right), 33 (bottom right), 101 (left), 103, 104, 108 (bottom left), 119
© **Reinhard Brucker:** Pages 11 (left), 47 (right), 106, 108 (bottom right), 112, 120
© **Lynn M. Stone:** Page 11 (right)
Photri: Pages 51, 63, 86 (middle), 128 (Hemingway), 129 (Lincoln), 131 (Sandburg); © A. Novak: Page 13
Journalism Services: © Jim Legault: Page 15; © Paul Burd: Page 77 (left); © Gregory Murphey: Page 82; © John Patsch: Pages 88, 99 (top left); © Mike Kidulich: Page 96 (inset)
Root Resources: © James Blank: Page 4 © Betty A. Kubis: Page 16 (bottom)
Nawrocki Stock Photo: Pages 47 (left), 51 (far left); © Phylan Norman, page 18 (top left and bottom right); © Terry Vitacco, page 18 (top right); © William S. Nawrocki, page 18 (bottom left); © Janet Davis, pages 19 (top right), 22 (bottom left), 24; © D.J. Variakojis, page 22 (right); © Robert Pickering, page 28; © Robert Lightfoot III, pages 31, 95; © Myron Davis, page 51 (top middle, middle right, and bottom); © Les Van, Page 72; © Candee, page 90; © Robert AMFT, page 92 (left)
Marilyn Gartman Agency: © Eric Futran Photography, page 18 (middle left); © Lee Balterman, pages 19 (top left), 66 (top right, bottom left, and bottom right), 102, 126 (Daley); © Carl E. Krupp, page 19 (middle right); © Diane Schmidt, page 117
Tom Stack & Associates: © Don & Pat Valenti: Page 5 © Gary Milburn, Pages 78-79; © Rick Myers, Page 68
The Image Bank: © D. William Hamilton, page 25
© **J.B. Nelson:** Page 26
Image Finders: © R. Flanagan, pages 29 (courtesy Ill. State Museum), 101 (right)
Historical Pictures Service, Inc., Chicago: Pages 33 (left), 34, 37 (left), 38-39, 42, 43, 45, 48, 53, 55 (left), 59, 66 (top left), 125, 126 (Blackhawk and Darrow), 127 (Dirksen, Douglas, and Fermi), 128 (Field), 129 (Lindsay, Masters, and McCormick), 130 (Mies van der Rohe, Palmer, and Rosenwald), 131 (Stevenson and Sullivan), 132
Chicago Historical Society: Pages 33 (top right: Ambrotype); page 37 (right: ICHi-14160), 55 (right), 56 (right: ICHI-09369), 58 (left: ICHi-04914), 58 (right: ICHi-00479), 61 (Jan Fujita/photographer), 86 (left: DN 94,246), 86 (right: DN 9914), 124 (DN 64,935), 127 (Du Sable: ICHI-12365), 130 (Monroe: DN 4359)
Hillstrom Stock Photos: © Arthur Brown 1986: Pages 51 (top right), 64 (right), 81 (right), 83 (left), 131 (Terkel)
© **Cameramann International Ltd.:** Pages 22 (top left), 56 (left), 64 (left), 71, 77 (right), 81 (left), 99 (bottom), 100, 121, 141
© **Stock Imagery:** Page 96-97
© **Joan Dunlop:** Pages 99 (top right), 108 (middle)
© **Richard L. Capps:** Page 108 (top left)
EKM-Nepenthe: Page 128 (Grant)
© **Johnson Publishing Company:** Page 128 (Johnson)
Wide World Photos: Page 126 (Brooks)
© **Joseph Antos,** Page 138
Len W. Meents: Maps on pages 100, 102, 104, 106, 136
Courtesy Flag Research Center, Winchester, Massachusetts 01890: Flag on page 108